Secretarial Contacts

Secretarial Contacts

Communication skills for secretaries and personal assistants

Nick Brieger and Anthony Cornish

Prentice Hall

New York London Toronto Sydney Tokyo Singapore

Published by
Prentice Hall Europe
Campus 400, Maylands Avenue
Hemel Hempstead
Hertfordshire, HP2 7EZ
A division of
Simon & Schuster International Group

Printed and bound in Great Britain by
Redwood Books, Trowbridge, Wiltshire.

Library of Congress Cataloging-in-Publication Data

Brieger, Nick.
Secretarial contacts: communication skills for
secretaries and personal assistants / Nick
Brieger, Anthony Cornish.
p.   cm.
1. English language – Conversation and
phrase books (for secretaries) 2. English
language – Textbooks for foreign speakers.
3. English language – Business English.
4. Office practice – Terminology. I. Cornish,
Anthony, 1961–   . II. Title.
PE1116.S42B75   1989
428.3′4′024651 – dc 19   88-38791

British Library Cataloguing in Publication Data

Brieger, Nick.
Secretarial contacts: communication skills for
secretaries and personal assistants.
1. English language – Questions and answers
– for secretaryship
I. Title   II. Cornish, Anthony, 1961–
428

ISBN 0-13-798638-6

10 11 12 13 14   01 00 99 98

Contents

Acknowledgements

Our thanks to Sarah Haggas of Human Resources, Cambridge, for her help and advice in the researching of this book.

Introduction

Rationale

The materials are aimed at students who are either in, or training for, posts as secretaries or personal assistants. In addition, they provide practice for students taking the London Chamber of Commerce and Industry examinations.

More specifically the materials are designed for learners at a pre-intermediate level or above, who need to develop the skills of listening, speaking, reading and writing in secretarial contexts. Each unit has a language focus, which highlights and practises language appropriate to the secretarial world, as follows:

Secretarial jobs and duties.
Reception.
Office equipment.
Office procedures.
Business meetings.
Face-to-face and telephone messages and arrangements.
Social communication.

Listening passages and reading texts act as input for tasks, focusing on both informational content and language content. In turn, this input is used as the basis for output tasks, focusing on the speaking and writing skills.

The listening and reading materials are based around:

Face-to-face dialogues.
Telephone calls.
Dictations.
Letters and memos.
Agendas.
Reports.

They develop the skills of:

Extracting relevant information.
Structuring information.
Inferring meaning from context.
Becoming accustomed to different varieties of English.

The follow-up speaking activities develop face-to-face and telephone communication skills, and the writing activities give practice in the composition and formulation of letters, telexes, memos and notes.

Organisation of the material

There are 26 units (see Contents page).
Each unit consists of the following:

Introduction

A short written introduction to the topic of the unit, often introducing key vocabulary.

1. **Listening/reading**

   A taped listening passage and/or reading text, accompanied by an information transfer task.

2. **Presentation**

   Highlighting and explanation of language items from the listening passage.

3. **Controlled practice**

   Exercises designed to practise the language items introduced in the Presentation.

4. **Transfer**

   Oral and/or written activities designed to encourage the students to use the language in a freer context.

5. **Word check**

   A glossary of the secretarial vocabulary that appears in the listening and reading passages.

In the second part of the book is a Key section for each unit. This contains the following:

1. **Listening/reading**

   A tapescript to the listening text and answers to the information transfer exercise.

3. **Controlled practice**

   Answers to the controlled practice exercise(s).

4. **Transfer**

   Information for pair work activities and suggested keys to the writing activities.

In the third part of the book are the Appendices. These contain the following:

1. **Telephone**

   The Telephone language appendix provides useful phrases for making and receiving calls.

2. Telex

The Telex appendix provides a list of telex short forms together with their expanded forms.

3. Abbreviations

The Abbreviations appendix provides a list of abbreviations in current use in business communication together with their expanded forms and meanings.

4. Letters

The Letter appendix provides models of business letters to which students should refer when doing a written transfer activity.

5. Vocabulary index

The Vocabulary index at the back of the book provides an alphabetical list of all words which appear in the unit glossaries (Word check) and the unit numbers of their appearances.

Teacher's notes

Uses of the material

1. As a complete course for secretaries who need English.
2. As supplementary material to a general English course for students with an interest in or a need for secretarial English.
3. As extensive course material for the English component in a secretarial training course.
4. As a self-study/homework component for a secretarial English course.
5. As follow-up material on completion of a secretarial English course.

Selection of material

The units are not graded, but there is a theme running through the book. Teachers may, therefore, select according to:

1. topic (see Contents page);
2. language area (see Contents page).

Using a unit

Introduction

You can use the text as a basis for presenting the unit orally or for asking students to read it through themselves.

1. Listening/reading

The input text for each unit may be either a listening passage and/or a reading passage.

(a) Prepare the students for the task. Make sure they are absolutely sure what they have to do.
(b) In the case of listening, play the tape right through without stopping; in the case of reading, ask the students to read the whole text.
(c) For many students it will be necessary to give them an opportunity to listen to the tape or read the text again. In the case of listening passages, stop the tape at appropriate places.
(d) Let the students check their answers with the Key.
(e) Play the tape again or ask the students to read the text again if there are major differences between the Key and the student answers.
(f) Refer the students to the Word check (section 5) if there are vocabulary problems.

2. Presentation

(a) Ask the students to read through the presentation and explanation of the language area.

(b) Get them to give you additional examples of the language presented.
(c) If necessary, look at the tapescript in the Key or the text in the student section to identify exponents of the language.

3. Controlled practice

(a) Ask the students to complete the exercises and then check their answers with the Key.
(b) Advise on alternative answers or give more practice where necessary.

4. Transfer

Some of these activities involve speaking and some writing. Most of the speaking activities involve pair work.

(a) Divide the class into pairs.
(b) Assign roles (Student A and Student B). Make sure they only look at their role/information (Student B's information is always in the Key section).
(c) Monitor the pairs while they carry out the speaking transfer, prompting the use of practised language if necessary. Correct written transfer activities, and then refer students to the model answer in the Key.

5. Word check

This can be used during the listening or reading activity. The glossary only provides definitions.

NOTE
The following symbols have been used to indicate what is missing in the exercises:

_ _ _ _ _   one or more words;
_____   only one word.

Notes to the student

Who is it for?

This material is for students who have some previous knowledge of English and wish to apply it in a secretarial context. It can be used by students working alone; as self-study or homework during a secretarial course; or as follow-up after a secretarial course.

Selection of material

You can work through the material starting at Unit 1. Alternatively, you can choose units on the basis of the topic or language area (see Contents page).

Using a unit

All of the units can be done without a teacher. All the sections in a unit can also be done without a teacher except for the spoken transfer activities.

Introduction

This tells you something about the subject of the unit.

1. Listening/reading

All the listening and reading activities have an exercise with them.

(a) Read through the introduction to the listening and/or reading. Make sure you understand what you have to do while you are listening or reading.
(b) In the case of listening, play the tape right through, without stopping; in the case of reading, read the whole text.
(c) As you listen or read, try to do the exercise.
(d) If necessary listen to the tape or read the text again. In the case of listening, stop the tape and replay sections if you need to.
(e) Check your answers with the Key at the back of the book.
(f) If your answers are wrong, listen or read again. You can check the tapescript in the Key. Use the Word check if you cannot understand some of the words.

2. Presentation

(a) Read carefully through the presentation and explanation of the language area.
(b) Try to remember how this language was used on the tape or in the text. If you wish, listen to the tape or read the text again.

3. Controlled practice

(a) Complete the exercises.
(b) Check your answers with the Key.
(c) If your answers are wrong, look again at the Presentation, and try to see why you have made mistakes.

4. Transfer

Some of these activities involve speaking and some writing. You can do the writing activities and pair work speaking activities without a teacher. However, the transfer activities are best done with a teacher who can correct your spoken and written language.
 If you do the pair work speaking activities with a colleague, follow this procedure:

(a) Decide who is Student A and who is Student B.
(b) Student A should *only* look at the Student A copy.
(c) Student B should *only* look at the Student B copy in the Key section.
(d) Carry out the Transfer activity. Try to use the language you have learnt.

5. Word check

The words are taken from the listening or reading passages. Try to think how you could use these words yourself.

NOTE
We have used the following symbols. They show you what is missing in the exercises:

_ _ _ _ _   one or more words;
_____   only one word.

UNIT 1   Job advertisements and applications

(stating requirements)

Introduction

In this unit Hilary Beacham and Erica Davidson consider two advertisements for the post of Personal Assistant/Secretary. The advertisements have appeared in the 'Secretarial vacancies' section of their local newspaper.

1a.   Reading

The advertisements below show what is:

    (a) necessary;
    (b) not necessary;
    (c) prohibited.

As you read through the advertisements, indicate the requirements in the appropriate column in the table below. The first one has been done for you.

COMPACT SYSTEMS

Personal Assistant/Secretary

required to assist departmental managers in our Southtown office. Applicants must have experience of working in a computer company and mustn't have less than ten years' job experience. Typing and shorthand preferred. Age: 30 + . Salary: £8,500 p.a. The job does not involve any travel.
    Candidates must provide a c.v., the names of two referees, and a statement of what makes a good PA/Secretary. Applications should be sent to:

        Compact Systems,
        96 Rosewall Drive,
        Southtown,
        SO3 4BT.

INVENTOR PLUS

Personal Assistant/Secretary to the Managing Director

We are looking for a suitably qualified person with a minimum of 5 years' experience of working in a business environment, but not necessarily in the computer industry, to take up a post as a Personal Assistant to the Managing Director. Applicants must have typing and shorthand skills, be well-dressed and willing to travel. Maximum age: 28. Full c.v. and the name of previous employer to:

        Inventor Plus,
        60 Chiswick Avenue,
        Southtown,
        SO3 6QZ.

	COMPACT SYSTEMS			INVENTOR PLUS		
	NECESSARY	NOT NECESSARY	PROHIBITED	NECESSARY	NOT NECESSARY	PROHIBITED
have experience of working in a computer company	✔					
have typing and shorthand skills						
have a minimum of five years' work experience						
have two referees						
be willing to travel						
send a full c.v.						
be under 28						

1b. Listening 🔘

Having seen the advertisements in the newspaper, Hilary and Erica start to discuss them in terms of:

   experience and qualifications required;
   method of application.

To apply for the job at Compact Systems, candidates must 'provide a statement of what makes a good PA/Secretary'. As you listen make a list of five things that Erica and Hilary think make a good PA/Secretary. The first one has been done for you.
1. Have a good filing system.
2.
3.
4.
5.

🔘

2. Presentation

Here is some of the language you have just read and heard. Notice some of the ways to express what is:

(a) necessary;
(b) not necessary;
(c) prohibited.

Necessary	Not necessary	Prohibited
must have to have got to	needn't/don't need to don't have to haven't got to	mustn't

E.g. Applicants must have experience of working in a computer company (written regulations and orders).
A good PA must distribute work fairly to other typists.
You have to have a good filing system (external obligation).
You've got to have a good phone manner (informal).

3. Controlled practice

Now look at the requirements for candidates wishing to apply for Personal Assistant jobs at the two companies below. Use the table below to make sentences about their requirements. The first one has been done for you.

REQUIREMENTS	EXPO			IMPO		
	NECESSARY	NOT NECESSARY	PROHIBITED	NECESSARY	NOT NECESSARY	PROHIBITED
Be able to work at weekends	✓				✓	
Be prepared to travel overseas		✓		✓		
Know how to use a computer	✓			✓		
Be over 30			✓	✓		
Speak German	✓				✓	

3

Expo
1. Candidates <u>must</u> <u>be</u> <u>able</u> <u>to</u> <u>work</u> <u>at</u> <u>weekends</u>.
2. Candidates don't _.
3. Candidates have _.
4. Candidates _.
5. Candidates _ _ _ _ _ _ _ got _ _ _ _ _ _ _ _ _ _ _ _ _ _ _.

Impo
6. Candidates _ _ _ _ _ need to _ _ _ _ _ _ _ _ _ _ _ _ _ _ _.
7. Candidates have _.
8. Candidates must _ _ _ _ _ _ _ _ _ _ _ _ _ _ _ _ _ _ _.
9. Candidates _ _ _ _ _ _ to _ _ _ _ _ _ _ _ _ _ _ _ _ _ _ _ _.
10. Candidates _ _ _ _ _ _ _ _ speak German.

COMPACT SYSTEMS
96 Rosewall Drive, Southtown, SO3 4BT

12 January 19____

63 Wenwell Gardens
Southtown
SO9 7PX

Dear _ _ _ _ _

I am writing in response to your advertisement for a Personal Assistant/Secretary _ _ _ _ _
_ _.

I am enclosing _
_ _ _ _ _ _ _ _ _ of my qualifications and experience. As you will see I have had
12 years' _ _ _ _ _ _ _ _ _ _ _ _ _ _, including two in _ _ _ _ _ _ _. I
also have an RSA* Stage III in Typing and RSA* 100 w.p.m. Shorthand.

In my opinion a good PA/Secretary must:

_ _ _ _ _ _ _ _ _ _ _ _ _ _ _
_ _ _ _ _ _ _ _ _ _ _ _ _ _ _
_ _ _ _ _ _ _ _ _ _ _ _ _ _ _
_ _ _ _ _ _ _ _ _ _ _ _ _ _ _
_ _ _ _ _ _ _ _ _ _ _ _ _ _ _

I will be _ _ _ _ _ _ _ _ _ _ _ _ _ _ _ _ _ _ _
_ _.

_ _ _ _ _ _

Hilary Beacham (signature)

Hilary Beacham

Note:
*RSA is the Royal Society of Arts, which offers secretarial qualifications in different subjects at different levels.

4. Transfer

Hilary has decided to write a letter to Compact Systems to apply for the job as Personal Assistant/Secretary. Draft a letter of application for her. Your letter should include a statement of what makes a good PA/Secretary, based on the information in 1b. Listening.
Before you do this activity, look at the model letter of application in Appendix 4, p. 171.

5. Word check

vacancy – job which is not filled
to require – to need
to assist – to help
shorthand – a system for writing letters, words and phrases quickly using a system of signs or short forms
application – an official letter requesting a job
to apply (for a job) – to request (something) officially, normally in writing
filing (system) – method of organising and storing papers, letters and other documents
to receive (visitors) – to greet people and make them welcome
to create a bad impression – to act in such a way that someone else thinks badly of you
to distribute – to divide among several or many people
neat – showing care in appearance

The interview

(asking for information and WH questions)

Introduction

Hilary Beacham decided to apply for the job of Personal Assistant/Secretary at Compact Systems. So she sent her c.v., the names of two referees, and a covering letter giving her ideas about 'what makes a good PA/Secretary'. A few days later she received a reply inviting her for interview.

1. Listening 🔘 ──────────────────────────

Listen to the following interview at Compact Systems. As you listen, complete the missing parts of Hilary's c.v.

CURRICULUM VITAE

PERSONAL
Name: _ _ _ _ _ _ _ _ _ _
Address: 63 Wenwell Gardens
_ _ _ _ _ _ _ _

Date of birth: _ _ _ _ _
Marital status: _ _ _ _ _

EDUCATION

*GCE 'O' LEVELS: _ _ _ _ _ _ _ _ _
Mathematics
Biology
Geography

**RSA: _ _ _ _ _ _ _ _ _ _ _ _ _
_ _ _ _ _ _ _ _ _ _ _ _ _

PROFESSIONAL EXPERIENCE

Company	Position	Length of service	Reason for leaving
1. _ _ _ _ _ _ _	_ _ _ _ _ _ _	_ _ _ _ _ _ _	_ _ _ _ _ _
2. _ _ _ _ _ _ _	_ _ _ _ _ _ _	_ _ _ _ _ _ _	_ _ _ _ _ _

Notes:
*GCE 'O' Level is the General Certificate in Education Ordinary level − an examination taken in different subjects at secondary school at about the age of 16. (This examination has now been superseded by GCSE.)
**RSA is the Royal Society of Arts which offers secretarial qualifications in different subjects at different levels.

---

2. Presentation

Below is a list of the WH question words which you have heard in the interview. Notice how they are used to ask for different types of information.

Question word	Information requested
Who?	people
What?	thing
When?	time
Where?	place
Why?	reason
How long?	length of time
How?	manner
How much/many?	quantity and amount

Here are some examples from the interview of the use of these WH question words.

Who did you work for there?
What secretarial qualifications did you get while you were at college?
And when did you start there?
Where did you work before Format?
And why did you leave that job?
And how long did you work at Ideal Systems?
So how much experience do you have of working in computer companies?

3. Controlled practice

Below is a list of answers to questions. Write a question which focuses on the underlined information in each answer. The first one has been done for you.

1. Q When did you start working for Compass?
   A I started working for them three years ago.

2. Q _ _ _ _ _ _ _ _ _ _ _ _ _ _
   A I got my secretarial qualifications in 1962.

3. Q _ _ _ _ _ _ _ _ _ _ _ _ _ _ _ _ _
   A I left my last job because I wanted to move to London.

4. Q _ _ _ _ _ _ _ _ _ _
   A I travelled to work by bus.

5. Q _ _ _ _ _ _ _ _ _ _ _ _ _ _ _
   A I worked for the Managing Director, George Tebbit.

6. Q _ _ _ _ _ _ _ _ _ _
   A I lived there for three years.

7. Q _ _ _ _ _ _ _ _ _ _
   A The meeting lasted three hours.

8. Q _ _ _ _ _ _ _ _ _ _
   A I studied typing and shorthand.

9. Q _ _ _ _ _ _ _ _ _ _ _
   A I usually typed about ten letters a day.

10. Q _ _ _ _ _ _ _
    A I worked at EXPO.

4. Transfer

■ PAIR WORK
You are now going to practise asking your partner interview questions to collect educational and professional information.

Student B: turn to the Key section.

Student A: below is a c.v. giving a brief outline of your education and career. Your partner is going to ask you questions. Answer the questions using the information below.

CURRICULUM VITAE

PERSONAL
Name: Mary Bailey
Date of birth: 17 December 1957
Marital status: Married

EDUCATION

Dates	Institutions
1968–1974	Ashton Secondary School
1974–1978	Ashton Secretarial College

Secretarial qualifications

Dates	Qualifications
1978	RSA Stage I Typing
1979	RSA Stage I Accounting
1980	RSA 60 w.p.m. Shorthand
1981	RSA Stage II Typing
1984	RSA Word-processing Diploma

PROFESSIONAL EXPERIENCE

Company	Position	Length of service	Reason for leaving
1. Partco	Secretary	4 years	Offer of better job
2. Webster	PA	3 years	Redundancy

Student A: ask your partner questions about him/herself in order to complete the brief c.v. below.

CURRICULUM VITAE

PERSONAL
Name: _____
Date of birth: _____
Marital status: _____

EDUCATION

Dates   Institutions

_____ – _____   _____
_____ – _____   _____

Secretarial qualifications
Dates   Qualifications

_____   _____
_____   _____
_____   _____
_____   _____
_____   _____

PROFESSIONAL EXPERIENCE

Company   Position   Length of service   Reason for leaving

1. _____   _____   _____

2. _____   _____   _____

---

5. Word check

c.v. (curriculum vitae) — summary of a person's life-story showing details of education and work experience
to go into liquidation — when a company stops trading, it goes into liquidation
customer — a person who buys goods or services from a shop or company
supplier — a person who provides goods or services
qualification — a proof that one has passed examinations and gained a certain degree of ability
software — computer programs on disk

Day 1: Meeting office staff

(introductions and greetings)

Introduction

Compact Systems interviewed six candidates for the post of Personal Assistant/Secretary. They made up their minds quite quickly, and decided to offer Hilary the job. They asked her to start the following Monday, and she agreed.

1. Listening 🔘🔘 ————————————————————

Hilary has just arrived at Compact Systems. As it's her first day, and she hasn't had a chance to meet her colleagues yet, Sheila Polson, the Personnel Manager, introduces her to some of the staff.

  As you listen, draw lines to link the name on the left with his/her position on the right. Then listen again and indicate in the left-hand column whether the greeting is formal (F) or informal (I). The first one has been done for you.

F	Alice Everett	Office Manager
	Christine Adams	Personal Assistant to Alice Everett
	Sally Hobday	Filing clerk
	Helen Wright	Marketing Manager
	George Brown	Secretary to Alice Everett
	Karen Williams	Secretary

🔘🔘

---

2. Presentation

a. Introductions between speakers normally follow a number of steps, as follows:

Person A
Introduction: How do you do?
Identification: My name is _____

Person B
Reply to introduction: Pleased to meet you.
Identification: I'm _____.

Now here is some of the language you have just heard.

(i) Introducing and identifying yourself

Formal: How do you do? I'm _____
           How do you do? My name's _____
Informal: Hello, my name's _____

10

(ii) Replying to introductions and identifying yourself

Formal: How do you do? I'm _____
How do you do? My name's _____
Pleased to meet you. My name's _____
Informal: Hello, my name's _____
Nice to meet you. My name's _____

(iii) Introducing someone else

Formal: I'd like to introduce you to _____
Can I introduce you to _____?
Let me introduce you two. _____, this is _____.
Informal: _____, this is _____.

b. Greetings between speakers also normally follow a number of steps, as follows:

Greeting	*Enquiry*	*Reply to enquiry*	*Enquiry*
Hello	How are you?	Fine, thanks	And you?

Now here is some of the language you have just heard.

(i) Greetings, enquiries and replies

Formal: Good morning, _____. How are you?
Very well, thank you. And you?
Informal: Hello, _____. How are you doing?
Fine, thanks. And you?

3. Controlled practice

Refer to the Presentation and complete these dialogues.

1. Greet your boss when you meet him in the evening.
   '_ _ _ _ _, Mr Simmons. How are you?'
   'Very well, thank you. _ _ _ _ _?'
2. Introduce your boss to a customer.
   '_ _ _ _ _ to introduce you to Mr Hampshire.'
   'Pleased to meet you. _ _ _ _ _ _ Askwith, Susan Askwith.'
3. Introduce a friend to another friend.
   'Paul, _ _ _ _ _ Erica.'
   '_ _ _ _ _.'
4. Greet Peter, a friend, at a party.
   '_ _ _ _ _, Peter. _ _ _ _ _?'
   '_ _ _ _ _. _ _ _ _ _?'
5. Introduce yourself to someone at a party.
   '_ _ _ _ _, my name's Paula.'
   '_ _ _ _ _. Mine's Gordon.'
6. Introduce yourself to a new customer.
   '_ _ _ _ _? I'm Harriet Arnold.'
   '_ _ _ _ _. _ _ _ _ _ Brown, Michael _ _ _ _ _.'
7. Introduce your boss to a client.
   'Let _ _ _ _ _. Mr Bryce, _ _ _ _ _ Mr Derry.'

4. Transfer

■ PAIR WORK

(a) Take it in turns to introduce yourself to your partner in the following situations:

   (i) at a formal reception for customers;
   (ii) at a friendly party.

(b) Now practise greeting your partner in the same two situations.

■ GROUP WORK

(c) Work in groups of three. Each member of the group should introduce the other two members of the group to each other in the same two situations.

5. Word check

filing clerk – a person whose job is to organise papers, letters and other documents for storage

staff – people who work for a company

boss – a person who has control over others

Office Manager – a person who controls the work in an office

office equipment – the machines used in an office, e.g., typewriters, word processors, photocopiers, etc.

Day 1: Getting to know the equipment

(identifying equipment and describing its function)

Introduction

Hilary Beacham spends her first day at Compact Systems with Christine Adams, the Office Manager. Christine shows Hilary the office equipment that she will need to use. At the end of the day Christine gives Hilary an office equipment manual, and asks her to read some of the sections to make sure that she understands the different items of equipment and their function.

1. Reading

Below are four sections from the office equipment manual. Each section identifies and describes an item of office equipment. While you are reading complete the chart at the end of the reading passages.

1.1. Word processors

This is a word processor:

A word processor displays the text you are typing on a screen. Manufacturers often refer to it as a 'screen typewriter'.

Recently, word processors have become increasingly important, and in many companies have almost totally replaced traditional typewriters.

The advantages are clear: a typist can see the whole text on the screen so the format can be changed and mistakes corrected before the document is printed. It is also easy and quick to correct mistakes.

1.2. Audio typing equipment

1.2.1. A dictating machine

This is a very useful facility in an office. It is used for recording letters onto magnetic tape for transcription by a secretary. The advantage of this for secretaries is that they don't need to take dictation — they are simply given a tape to transcribe when it is convenient.

1.2.2. A remote dictation system
This is a remote dictating machine:

It has the same function as a normal desktop dictating machine, but it has the added advantage of being portable — it can be used on a train, a plane, etc.

1.3. Telex machines

This is a telex machine:

The function of a telex machine is very simple: it is used for sending and receiving messages on the telephone system. The advantages of this are that it is available day and night and it is also inexpensive.

1.4. Facsimile machines (fax)

This is a facsimile machine (fax):

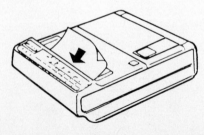

The facsimile machine, or 'fax', is an important addition to the modern office. It is for sending copies of documents, pictures, diagrams, etc., and it's obviously much quicker than posting.

Equipment	Function	Advantage(s)
1. Word processor	displays _____ on a _____	(i) you can see the whole text (ii) easy and _____ to _____ _____
2. Dictating machine	it is _____ for recording _____ onto _____	(i) secretaries don't _____ to _____ _____
3. Telex	it is used _____ _____ and receiving _____	(i) _____ day and _____ (ii) inexpensive
4. Facsimile machine	it is _____ _____ copies of documents, pictures, etc.	(i) _____ _____ posting

2. Presentation

Here is some of the language you have just read. Notice how it is used to identify and describe the function of equipment.

IDENTIFYING EQUIPMENT	DESCRIBING ITS FUNCTION
This is a word processor	It displays text on a screen
This is a facsimile machine	It is for sending copies of documents, etc.
This is a telex machine	It is used for sending and receiving messages

Notes:
'It is for —ing' describes the function of a piece of equipment, e.g. it is for sending copies.
'It is used for —ing' also describes the function of a piece of equipment, e.g. it is used for recording letters onto tape.
We also use the present simple to describe the function of a piece of equipment, e.g. it displays text on the screen.

Things can have more than one function. If we want to explain that something has two functions, we say:

FUNCTION 1
It's used for typing documents and

FUNCTION 2
(it's used for) displaying them on a screen.

3. Controlled practice

In the table below you have a number of items of office equipment on the left and their function on the right.

First identify the function of each item of office equipment by writing the appropriate number by the expression which describes its function.

Then complete the sentences below using the information from the table. The first sentence identifies the equipment; the second sentence describes its function.

The first one in each case has been done for you.

Equipment	Function
(1) stapler	( ) stick one piece of paper to another.
(2) hole punch	(1) fix pieces of paper together.
(3) ruler	( ) make holes in paper stronger.
(4) Tippex fluid	( ) erase mistakes.
(5) paper clips	( ) make holes in paper.
(6) reinforcement rings	( ) correct mistakes.
(7) paper glue	( ) draw straight lines.
(8) rubber	( ) sharpen pencils.
(9) pencil sharpener	( ) hold pieces of paper together.

1. This is a stapler. It is used for fixing pieces of paper together.
2. This __ __ __ __ __. __ __ __ __ __ makes __ __ __ __ __.
3. This __ __ __ __ __. __ __ __ __ __ used __ __ __ __ __.
4. This __ __ __ __ __. __ __ __ __ __ is for __ __ __ __ __.
5. These __ __ __ __ __. __ __ __ __ __ hold __ __ __ __ __.
6. __ __ __ __ __ are __ __ __ __ __. __ __ __ __ __ used __ __ __ __ __.
7. __ __ __ __ __ is __ __ __ __ __. __ __ __ __ __ is for __ __ __ __ __.
8. This __ __ __ __ __. It __ __ __ __ __.
9. This __ __ __ __ __. __ __ __ __ __ used __ __ __ __ __.

4. Transfer

■   GROUP WORK

For this activity you are going to work in groups of six. First each group should select twenty different items of office equipment. One person in the group should then write the items down. Each item must be on a separate small piece of card or paper.

Next the groups exchange their cards. The group receiving the cards must not look at them. Each group then places their new cards face down in the middle of the table. One member of the group then takes the first card. He/she looks at what is written on the card, but must not show it to anyone else.

The other members of the group have to ask questions about its function; the person holding the card can only answer 'yes' or 'no'. When someone guesses the item written on the card, that person then takes the next card; the others have to ask questions about its function to guess its identity. The winner is the person with the most cards.

You should ask questions about the function of the item, as follows:

Is it used for _____?
Is it for _____?

Remember that the person holding the card can only answer 'yes' or 'no'.

5. Word check

manual − a book giving information or instructions
section − part of a book, manual, etc.
to display − to show
screen − front of a display unit (or TV) on which you can see information
traditional − old-fashioned
format − organisation or arrangement
facility − (piece of equipment which gives you) the ability to do something
transcription − the action of writing a copy
to transcribe − to write a copy
portable − can be carried

Who's who in the company

(classification)

Introduction

Hilary Beacham has now finished her induction into Compact Systems with Christine Adams, the Office Manager, and George Brown, the departing Personal Assistant to Alice Everett. It is the beginning of her second week, and today she is going to start two months' work as Personal Assistant to Alice Everett, the Marketing Manager.

1. Listening 〔∞〕

Alice Everett has decided to start by explaining to Hilary:

who is who in the company;
who is responsible for what in the company;
who everybody works for.

As you listen to the tape, complete the organisation flowchart below by filling in the missing job titles and name.

Compact Systems — company structure

Name: David Burton
Title: Managing Director
PA: Mary Wilkins

Name: Michael Stott	Name: Sheila Polson	Name: _____ _____	Name: Paul Cummins
Title: _____ _____	Title: _____ _____	Title: Marketing Manager	Title: _____ _____
PA: Daniel Harkin	PA: Jane Hargreaves	PA: Hilary Beacham	PA: Judith Walker
2 secretaries	2 secretaries	2 secretaries	3 secretaries

〔∞〕

2. Presentation

When you want to classify someone in a company, you can do so according to:

their responsibility;
their position in the hierarchy;
their job specification;
their location.

Here is some of the language you have just heard for each of the four areas.

A. Responsibility
1. Paul Cummins is responsible for the Finance Department.
2. Michael Stott looks after Production.

B. Position in the hierarchy
1. Jane Hargreaves works for the Personnel Manager.
2. Helen Wright and Karen Williams will report to you.
3. Emma Sharp works under Judith Walker.
4. Jane Williams works with Samantha Wolf (at the same level).

C. Job specification
1. David Burton is the Managing Director.
2. Daniel Harkin works as Personal Assistant.

D. Location
1. Anna Bartlett works in the Personnel Department.
2. Fran Tovey and Dorothy White are in the Finance Department.

3. Controlled practice

Now refer to the company structure in the listening section and complete the following sentences. The first one has been done for you.

---

1. Judith Walker <u>works as</u> Personal Assistant.
2. Paul Cummins _____ the Financial _____.
3. Jane Hargreaves _____ _____ the Personnel Director.
4. Two secretaries _____ _____ Daniel Harkin in the _____ _____.
5. Alice Everett _____ to the Managing Director.
6. Michael Stott _____ _____ _____ the Production Department.
7. Hilary Beacham _____ in the _____ Department.
8. Paul Cummins looks _____ the _____ Department.

---

4. Transfer

■ PAIR WORK
Student B: turn to the Key section.
Student A: (a) this is a diagram of the company structure of Whitney Industrials Inc. Use the language presented above to describe it to Student B. Student B is going to write the information in his/her flowchart.
After you have finished, compare your flowcharts.

Whitney Industrials

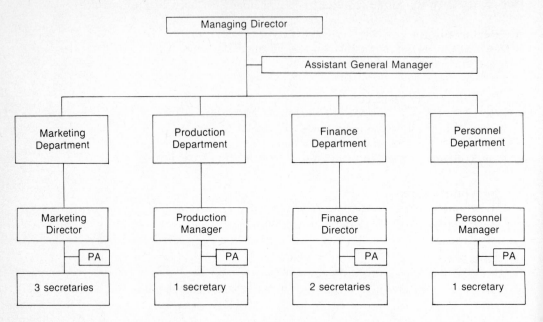

Managing Director

Assistant General Manager

Marketing Department	Production Department	Finance Department	Personnel Department
Marketing Director	Production Manager	Finance Director	Personnel Manager
PA	PA	PA	PA
3 secretaries	1 secretary	2 secretaries	1 secretary

(b) Your partner is now going to describe the structure of Wolverhampton Agrochem. Complete the diagram below.
After you have finished, compare your flowcharts.

Wolverhampton Agrochem

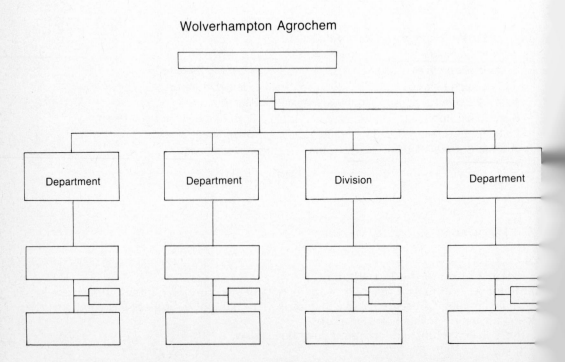

Department	Department	Division	Department

5. Word check

induction − period of introduction to a new job
department − a division or part of a company
Production Manager − person in charge of the Production Department
Personnel Manager − person in charge of the employees in a company and their
  conditions of work
Financial Manager − person in charge of a company's money matters
brief − short
overview − general picture

Checking arrangements

(telephoning 1)

Introduction

Compact Systems are arranging an international meeting to launch their new product range. Various companies have been invited, and Hilary now has to ring the companies up to check who is going to attend and when they are going to arrive.

1. Listening 🔲

Hilary has to make three international phone calls. Three representatives from foreign companies are coming to Compact Systems and Hilary has to find out their travel details. As you listen, fill in the table below.

	Phone call		
	1	2	3
Name:	Günther Harz	Ricardo Garniga	Martin Feldman
Arrival date:			
Airport:			
Airline:			
Flight number:			
Time:			

🔲

2. Presentation

Let's consider the phone calls made by Hilary in terms of the following steps:

    introductory procedures
    main part
    final procedures

Now let's look at the language used for the introductory and final procedures.

1. **Introductory procedures**
(a) Requesting your correspondent:
    Ricardo Garniga, please.
    Can/could I speak to _____, please?
(b) Identifying yourself:
    My name is Hilary Beacham from Compact Systems (first introduction).
    (This is) Hilary Beacham from Compact here (subsequent introductions).

(c) Explaining the purpose of your call:
   I'm ringing to check your travel details.
   I'm calling to find out your travel arrangements.

2. Final procedures
(a) Indicating that you've got all the relevant information:
   Well, that's all, Mr Feldman.
   I think that's all I need to know.
   That's all for now.
(b) Thanking your correspondent for the information:
   Thank you (very much).
   Thanks very much for the information.
(c) Final greeting:
   Goodbye.
   'Bye.

3. Controlled practice

Now put the following sentences from a phone call into the right order. The speakers are:

S   = Switchboard
SJ = Sally Jones
AP = Ann Pilkington

AP: Fine thanks, and you? ( )
S: Who's calling, please? ( )
AP: Well, thanks very much for the information. ( )

AP: Could I speak to Sally Jones, please? ( )
AP: Hello, Sally. This is Ann Pilkington here. ( )
SJ: Not at all. ( )
SJ: Oh, hello Ann. How are you? ( )
S: MIB. Good morning. (1)
AP: Sally, I'm ringing to ask if you can recommend a good ... ( )
AP: My name is Ann Pilkington. ( )
AP: 'Bye. ( )
SJ: Yes, fine, too. ( )
S: One moment, please. ( )
SJ: 'Bye. ( )
SJ: Sally Jones. ( )

4. Transfer

■ PAIR WORK

Student B: turn to the Key section.

(a) **Student A:** your boss has given you the following list of key participants for your company's annual international sales conference, and has asked you to check that the starred names are coming.
Ring the company and complete your table below.
Remember to:

   request your correspondent;
   identify yourself;
   explain the purpose of your call;
   thank your correspondent for the information;
   end the call.

Name	Company	Arrival date	Flight number	Time	Departure date	Flight number	Time
Harz, Günther	CTM	27 Feb.	LF 129	14.30	1 March	BA 306	17.30
Garniga, Ricardo	SC	26 Feb.	BA 322	10.00	1 March	IB 438	18.00
Feldman, Martin	IS	27 Feb.	TW 360	18.15	?	?	?
Walker, John*	ABT						
Roberts, Paul*	ABT						

(b) **Student A:** you work in the Scottish office of ABT. In this activity you will need to play two roles:

(i) the switchboard of ABT;
(ii) the PA/secretary who has just collected the air tickets below.

In the activity you need to carry out the following steps:

answer the phone and identify your company (from the switchboard)
find out the caller's identity (from the switchboard)
connect the caller (from the switchboard)
identify yourself (as PA/secretary)
give the relevant information (as PA/secretary)
end the call (as PA/secretary)

Itinerary prepared for: *Mr. George Lloyd*
Flight information: all times indicated are local

Date	Flight number	Airport check in	Time	Departure time	Arrival time
26 Feb	BA 127	Edinburgh	21.30	22.00	23.00
28 Feb	BA 126	London HR	19.45	20.15	21.15

Itinerary prepared for: *Mr. Eric Tober*
Flight information: all times indicated are local

Date	Flight number	Airport check in	Time	Departure time	Arrival time
28 Feb	BA 817	Edinburgh	06.00	06.30	07.30
2 March	BA 316	London HR	08.45	09.15	10.15

5. Word check

to launch — to put a new product on the market
to connect — to join by phone
to solve — to find an answer to a problem
short notice — information given a short time before an event happens
(hotel) reservation — booking

Booking a hotel room

(checking and correcting information)

Introduction

Alice Everett is abroad on company business, and has sent Hilary Beacham a telex asking her to make arrangements for an important meeting.

1a. Reading

Read the telex below which Alice Everett has sent to Hilary Beacham. Then indicate in the table below the five requirements which the hotel must satisfy.

```
ATTN HILARY BEACHAM

REF VISIT TO LONDON FOR MR CRAMER.   FIND SUITABLE HOTEL FOR 5, 6
AND 7 MAY.   PHONE ESSENTIAL + NEAR  LANCASTER ROAD.   MUST HAVE
MEETING ROOM + RESTAURANT.   ARRANGE AND CONF WITH ME.

RGDS
ALICE EVERETT
```

REQUIREMENTS
1. Room available 5th, 6th and 7th May
2.
3.
4.
5.

1b. Listening 🔲

Hilary phones three hotels in order to ask about their facilities and availability. Listen to the telephone calls. As you listen, indicate in the table below which hotels meet the requirements above (1–5). Write ✔ if the hotel meets the requirements, and write ✘ if it does not. Some have been done for you.

Requirements	Hotel 1	Hotel 2	Hotel 3
1.	✔		
2.			✔
3.		✗	
4.	✔		
5.			✔

2. Presentation

Checking information

There are several ways to check that you have heard or understood information correctly.
(a) Saying that you didn't hear correctly:
   Sorry, I didn't quite catch those dates.
(b) Asking for repetition:
   Could you repeat that, please?
(c) Asking for spelling:
   Can you spell that, please?
(d) Repeating the information:
   Did you say 'restaurant'?
(e) Repeating the first part of the information:
   The Goodwood: The 5th ...
   Hilary: ... 6th and 7th.

Correcting information

Excuse me. Not '60' — sixteen.
That's not quite right.
I'm afraid you've made a mistake.

3. Controlled practice

Here are seven statements which are wrong. After each statement the correct information is given in brackets. Correct each wrong statement, starting your answer with the word(s) given. The first one has been done for you.

1. The telephone number is 01-650 2703. (01-650 2037)
   That's not quite right. The number is 01-650 2037.

2. The flight leaves at 9.55. (9.58)
   I'm afraid _____ _____ _____ _____. The flight _____ _____
   _____.

3. There are going to be fifty people at the meeting. (15)
   Excuse _____. Not _____ — _____.

4. Mr Little lives at 206 North Parade. (South Parade)

I'm afraid _____ _____ _____ _____. Mr Little _____ _____
_____ _____ Parade.

5. The first letter is to Mr Dwight: D – W – I – G – H – T. (Dwite: D – W – I – T – E)
   That's _____ _____ _____. His name _____ _____: – – – – –.

6. The total profits for this year are £29,468. (£28,313)
   I'm afraid _____ _____ _____ _____. The total profits _____
   _____.

7. To get to the restaurant, go straight across the lights and turn second right. (third right)
   Excuse _____. Not _____ _____ – _____ right.

4. Transfer 🔲

Listen to the tape of the secretary taking dictation from her boss. Listen to them checking
and correcting information and complete the letter below.

Mr D.P. Broadham
116 Field Rise
Manchester

Dear _ _ _ _ _ _

_ _
_ _
_ _ _ _ _ _ _ _ _ _ _ _ _ _.

_ _
_ _
_ _
_ _ _ _ _ _ _ _ _ _ _ _ _ _ _ _ _ _.

_ _ _ _ _ _ _

S.M. Cork
Sales Manager

🔲

5. Word check

to speak up – to speak louder
bad line – when it is difficult to understand someone on the phone
location – position
(to be booked) solid – fully booked
off (Lancaster Road) – (a smaller road) connected to (Lancaster Road)

Transfer listening

postcode — group of letters and numbers added to an address on letters and parcels so that they can be delivered more quickly

overseas — abroad

invoice — request for payment

delivery — act of taking something (goods) to someone

Receiving visitors

(offering, accepting and declining hospitality)

Introduction

An important visitor has come to the office for an appointment with Alice Everett, the Marketing Manager. He is early, so Alice has asked Hilary to look after him until she's ready. Sally, one of the secretaries, is also in the office.

1. Listening

Listen to the conversation between Hilary and Mr Brown. As you listen, indicate in the table below whether Mr Brown accepts or declines the offers made by Hilary and Sally. The first one has been done for you.

Offer	Accept	Decline
to take Mr Brown's coat	✔	
to sit down		
to have a drink		
to call the hotel		
to call a taxi		
to have a biscuit		

2. Presentation

In the listening section Hilary and Sally offered hospitality, and Mr Brown accepted or declined. Now look at the language used:

Offers
Can I take your coat?
Shall I call a taxi?
Would you like to take a seat?
Would you like me to call them for you?

Accepting	**Declining**
Yes please.	No thanks/no thank you.
Yes, that's very kind of you.	Thank you, but it's not necessary.
Yes, that would be very nice.	Thank you, but no.

3. Controlled practice

Offer the following to a visitor. The first one has been done for you.

1. Drink something
   <u>Would you like to</u> drink something?

2. Take your coat
   _____ _____ take your coat?

3. Reserve a table for you.
   _____ _____ _____ _____ _____ reserve a table for you?

4. Take an earlier flight
   _____ _____ _____ _____ take an earlier flight?

5. Do anything else for you
   _____ _____ do anything else for you?

Now complete the following sentences with appropriate words to accept or decline the offer.

1. Can I get you a drink?
   _____ please.

2. Would you like a biscuit?
   _____ _____ you.

3. Would you like me to book a taxi?
   _____ _____, but _____.

4. Would you like to go to the theatre tonight?
   Yes, _____ _____ _____ _____ nice.

5. Would you like me to collect you from the hotel tomorrow?
   _____ you, but _____ _____ _____.

4. Transfer

■ PAIR WORK
Student B: turn to the Key section.

(a) **Student A:** It is 11 o'clock. Your boss (Mr Green) is expecting Mr/s Klein from Germany. You have been asked to look after him/her for a few minutes. When s/he arrives:

  introduce yourself;
  explain that your boss will be free in a few minutes;
  offer to take his/her coat;
  invite him/her to sit down;
  offer something to drink;
  make other appropriate offers according to Mr/s Klein's needs.

(b) **Student A:** It is 11 o'clock. You are Mr/s de Miguel from Spain. You have just arrived at your partner's company for an appointment with Mr Black. Now:

  introduce yourself;
  explain that you have an appointment with Mr Black;
  accept or decline the offers;
  explain you have another appointment at 3 o'clock;
  explain that you don't have a hotel reservation;
  explain that you need to change some money;
  explain that your luggage is still at the airport;
  explain that you need to confirm your return flight for tomorrow evening at 17.00.

5. Word check

to expect – to wait for someone as agreed
to take a seat – to sit down
to stretch one's legs – to stand, especially after sitting for a time (informal)
to sort out – to arrange
reservation – booking
to get through – to reach someone by phone
to call – to phone

Dealing with salesmen/representatives

(present simple and present continuous)

Introduction

In this unit Christine Adams, the Office Manager, meets two salesmen from two office supplies companies — Isis Office Equipment and Arco Office Supplies. The salesmen want to discuss Compact's requirements and try to get orders.

1. Listening 🔲

Compact have a standard form which Christine must fill in when salesmen visit the company. As you listen, fill in the forms.

Office supplies		
Company name: _ _ _ _ _ _ _ _ _		
Product	**Offer price**	**Features**
1. Ring binders 2. 3.		(i) (ii) good range of colours (i) (ii) (i) (ii) good reproduction

Office supplies		
Company name: _ _ _ _ _ _ _ _ _		
Product	**Offer price**	**Features**
1. Printer ribbons 2. 3.		(i) (ii) don't smudge (i) (ii) (i) (ii) don't corrupt

🔲

2. Presentation

Here is some of the language you have just heard. Notice how the different tenses are used.

PRESENT SIMPLE
Form
This tense is formed by using the infinitive of the verb (without 'to').
Remember the 's' after 'he', 'she', 'it' or a singular noun or pronoun,
e.g. Arco supplies most of our equipment.

Meaning
This tense is used when you want to talk about what people do all the time, or normally,
e.g. We buy from various sources.
    Do you use ring binders?

PRESENT CONTINUOUS
Form
This tense is formed by using is/am/are with the '—ing' form of the verb (e.g. 'making')
e.g. We are selling photocopying paper.

Meaning
It is used to talk about what people are doing now.
e.g. We are using the typewriters at the moment.
    I am running out of filing space.

3. Controlled practice

Complete the following passage with the correct form of the verb in brackets.

MEMORANDUM

To: All office staff   Subject: Redundancies
From: Personnel Officer   Date: 13th September

As you know the current rise in manufacturing costs ____(1)____(cause) a reduction in our profit margins. Normally, we ____(2)____(employ) fifty staff in the Personnel Department, but we ____(3)____(plan) to reduce the number of factory workers and therefore also the number of office staff. For these reasons the Managing Director ____(4)____(ask) for names of staff who would like to take early retirement.

Many people ____(5)____(complain) that we are presently understaffed, but at the moment we ____(6)____(try) to resolve the problems. On October 1st we will computerise the department, and I ____(7)____(think) you all know the probable consequences.

At the moment, I ____(8)____(try) to improve working conditions in the department, and at this difficult time I ____(9)____(need) your help in achieving these objectives.

---

4. Transfer

Student B: turn to the Key section.

(a) **Student A:** tell your partner about your normal duties in the company (i.e., what you regularly do in your job). Then tell your partner about the present situation, e.g. 'My

34

boss normally gives me a lot of letters to type, but he is visiting a client abroad at the moment.'

(b) Your partner is now going to tell you his/her normal duties in the company, and the present situation. Write notes in the table below.

Regular	Now

5. Word check

requirement — need
source — place where something comes from, supplier
competitor — person or company offering the same products or services as you
special deal — good offer (usually through a reduction in price)
catalogue — books showing products or services available
to stock — to keep a quantity of a product
introductory offer — special offer to a new customer or for a new product or service
reasonable (price) — fair or cheap
to smudge — to leave a dirty mark on a piece of paper
to corrupt — to change, add or delete (data)
storage capacity — the quantity of information that can be put onto a disk

Future engagements

(future reference)

Introduction

Alice Everett is abroad on a business trip. She has a marketing meeting in Manchester as soon as she returns, but the details had not been finalised before she left. She asked her secretary, Karen Williams, to arrange the rest of the details, and agreed to phone for the up-to-date information.

1. Listening 🔾🔾

As you listen, fill in the details in Alice Everett's diary.

19th October		
Time	**Place**	**Event**
	Le Manoir restaurant	Arrival Present new accountancy package

20th October		
Time	**Place**	**Event**
10.00 – 12.00 a.m.		

🔾🔾

2. Presentation

In the telephone conversation Alice Everett and Karen Williams discussed future arrangements.

The verb form to indicate the future depends on whether the speaker is talking about:
an intention;
a fixed plan or arrangement;
a fixed schedule.

Intention

e.g. I'm going to present our new accountancy package.
Form: 'to be going to' + infinitive
Meaning: It is *my intention* to present our new accountancy package.

Fixed plan or arrangement

e.g. What time are we having lunch on the 19th?
Form: present continuous
Meaning: What time is *our fixed arrangement* for lunch on the 19th?

Fixed schedule

e.g. It arrives at 9.30.
Form: present simple
Meaning: It is *the fixed schedule* (of the airline) that it arrives at 9.30.

3. Controlled practice

Below are some notes you have written to remind yourself about your future engagements. Some are intentions (indicated with a ?), some are fixed plans (indicated with a +), and some are fixed schedules (indicated with a + +). Use the notes to write sentences. The first one has been done for you.

1. 13ᵗʰ May / 12.00 / have lunch with JC (?)
   I am going to have lunch with JC on 13ᵗʰ May at 12.00

2. 14ᵗʰ May / morning / start training course (+)

3. 14ᵗʰ May / 17.00 / training course end (+ +)

4. 14ᵗʰ May / 19.30 / go theatre with PD (+)

5. 14ᵗʰ May / 17.30 / collect new dress (+ +)

6. 15ᵗʰ May / discuss training course with VE / and ask for rise (?)

7. VE say / she ask MD (?)

8. 16ᵗʰ May / have interview at PS (+)

9. 17ᵗʰ May / MD chat about the future (?)

10. 17ᵗʰ May / 12.00 / hand in notice (+ +)

4. Transfer

At the end of the listening task, Alice Everett asked Karen Williams to send a letter and telex to Mr Collins giving details of her two-day visit. Use the information from the Listening exercise to compose the letter and the telex. The letter should include all the details of the visit; the telex should only contain relevant times and places.

For guidance on letter layout see Appendix 4; for guidance on telex language see Appendix 2.

(a) Start your letter as follows:

COMPACT SYSTEMS

96 Rosewall Drive, Southtown, SO3 4BT

Mr K Collins
Regional Co-ordinator
Impact Systems
43 Wythenshawe Road
Manchester M21 4QD

————— 19——

Dear Mr Collins

I have now finalised the details of my visit to Manchester next week. __ __ __ __ __ __ __ __
__ __
__ __
__ __
__ __
__ __
__ __
__ __

Alice Everett
Marketing Manager

(b) Start your telex as follows:

```
ATTN: KEN COLLINS
FROM: ALICE EVERETT

RE: VISIT TO MANCHESTER 19 & 20 OCT.
```

5. Word check

abroad – foreign country
bad line – when it is difficult to hear someone on the phone
to sort out – to arrange
itinerary – timetable
due – expected
appointment – fixed meeting
package – collection of programs on a computer disk for a specific purpose, e.g. accountancy
to go off – to be posted

Conference facilities

(comparison and modification of adjectives)

Compact is arranging a two-day sales conference for its UK and European sales reps in Bath, in the south-west of England. It is rather short notice and David Burton has sent the following urgent memo to Alice Everett, and Alice has passed it on to Hilary Beacham.

Memo

28 August 19——

To: Alice Everett
From: David Burton

Subject: Sales conference

Urgent

I think we should hold the November Conference in a hotel this year. The travel between the different hotels and the Bath Conference Centre last year wasted a lot of time, so this year I suggest we have meetings and accommodation in the same venue. I have made a few preliminary enquiries from colleagues and they have given me the names of the following hotels:

Hotel International
The Regency
Bath Concord
The Imperial

(I hope I've got their names right).

Please keep me informed of developments.

---

1. Listening 🔲

Hilary has decided to start by phoning the Conference Information Centre in Bath to check the hotels on the memo.
   She has made a list below of the facilities and features which Alice has said are important.
   As you listen:

   write the name of the hotel
   indicate with a tick (✔) if the hotel has the feature indicated
   indicate with a cross (✗) if the hotel doesn't have the feature indicated

Some have been done for you.

	1. The International	2. ___	3. ___	4. ___
		Hotels		
large and small conference rooms	✗			
special rates in November				
near the city centre				
close to the airport		✔		
easy access by road				✗

2. Presentation

(a) In the telephone conversation the Information Officer compared the location and facilities of the hotels.
   In making these comparisons, he followed these rules:
    (i) One-syllable adjectives: add 'er',
       e.g. WIDE − They have a slightly wider choice.
    (ii) Two-syllable adjectives ending in 'ow', 'le' and 'y': add 'er',
       e.g. SIMPLE − It would be much simpler if I . . .
          EASY − Much easier than the Imperial.
       Other two-syllable and three-, four- and five-syllable adjectives: use 'more',
       e.g. EXPENSIVE − Their conference rooms are much more expensive.

(b) When describing the location and facilities of the hotels, the Information Officer also modified his adjectives, as follows:

With positive adjectives	*With comparative adjectives*
	slightly wider
	a little more
quite short	rather closer
pretty easy	somewhat more expensive
fairly close	
very easy	considerably closer
extremely large	much easier

3. Controlled practice

Look at the following extract about the location and facilities of the Imperial hotel. Select the most appropriate word(s) from the choice given.

Dear Guest,

We are not only more/very exclusive than our competitors, we are simply much/very better. As we are much/very sure that you have already noticed, the Imperial is located in a much/extremely good position and is easier/more easier to reach than other large hotels. Of course we are somewhat/quite big. Yet we feel that we still offer a very/considerably personal service to all our guests. And if we were smaller/more small, your choice of facilities would be much/more limited. And so our motto is 'Slightly/extremely more expensive/expensiver but slightly/considerably better'.

4. Transfer

■ PAIR WORK
Before starting this activity, you may wish to refer to the telephone language in Appendix 1.

Student B: turn to the Key section.

Student A: below are details of four hotels in Bath.

	The International (*****)	The Regent (****)	The Concord (***)	The Imperial (****)
Rooms	127	146	180	200
Restaurants	4	3	4	2
Distance to airport	16 miles	1 mile	3 miles	7 miles
Meeting rooms	2	4	10	12

(a) You work as Information Officer for the Bath Tourist Office. Use the information in the tables in the Controlled practice to answer Student B's questions.

(b) After Student B has collected the information s/he is going to check it by comparing the four hotels.

In each case Student B will try to say that there is a big difference, e.g.
'So The Concord is much bigger than The Regent?'
You should disagree in your reply by saying that there is a moderate or small difference, e.g.
'Well, in fact, The Concord is somewhat/slightly bigger than The Regent, rather than much bigger.'

Now you continue by disagreeing in your replies with Student B.

(c) Finally, Student B will tell you his/her requirements. Make a note of these so that you can help him/her to make the final choice.

5. Word check

conference — large meeting of people from the same professional area
facilities — equipment or buildings which make it easy to do something
to waste (time) — to use time badly
accommodation — place to sleep and eat
venue — place
preliminary — initial
enquiry — question
participant — person who takes part in something
access — way in, entrance
(special) rate — reduced price
off-season — not in the busiest time of the year
discount — reduced price
booklet — little book

Office talk

(present perfect)

___

Introduction

There's a new secretary in the Finance Department; there are plans for a new office, plans for holidays, and plans for new houses.

1. Listening 🎧

Listen to the conversation between Hilary Beacham and Karen, one of the secretaries. As you listen, fill in the table. If the answer to the question is 'yes', put ✔. If the answer is 'no', put ✗.

	Hilary	Karen
Met the new secretary in Finance	✔	
Seen the plans for the new extension		
Been to France		
Moved house		

___

2. Presentation

Here is some of the language you have just heard. Notice how the present perfect is used.
(a) The present perfect is used to indicate a non-specific time in the past, e.g.
Have you seen the plans?
I've heard they want to move all the departments around.
(b) The present perfect is used with 'already' and 'yet'.
'Already' is used in positive statements, e.g.
We've already packed everything up ...
'Yet' is used in questions when we expect a positive answer, e.g.
Have you seen her yet?
'Yet' is also used in negative statements, e.g.
The bosses haven't agreed on the details yet.
(c) The present perfect is used with 'since' and 'for' to indicate an action which started in the past and continues to the present.
'Since' introduces a starting point in the past, e.g.
I haven't been there since 1983.
'For' introduces a period of time, e.g.
I've known her for years.

3. Controlled practice

(a) Alice Everett has given the following checklist of actions to Hilary Beacham, and Hilary has written the present situation in the 'Status' column. What does Hilary say to Alice? The first one has been done for you.

Person	Action	Status
Hilary	Found the file on Bovis	No
Hilary	Sent off the new report	Yes
Hilary	Typed up the minutes of the last meeting	No
Karen	Circulated the agenda for the meeting	Yes
Karen	Sent the timesheets to Personnel	No

1. I haven't found the file on Bovis yet.
2. I've _____ _____ _____ the new report.
3. I _____ _____ _____ _____ _____ _____ the last meeting _____.
4. Karen _____ _____ _____ _____ agenda for the next meeting.
5. Karen _____ _____ the timesheets _____ _____ _____.

(b) Hilary also has some questions for Mrs Everett. What does she say? (In each case Hilary expects a positive answer.)

Person	Action
Mrs Everett	Found the file on Bovis.
Mrs Everett	Checked today's correspondence.
Karen	Brought the new catalogue.
Managing Director	Decided when the office staff will move.

1. Have you found the file on Bovis yet?
2. _____ you _____ _____ correspondence _____?
3. _____ Karen _____ _____ _____ catalogue _____?
4. _____ the Managing Director _____ _____ _____ _____ _____ will move _____?

(c) Hilary also wants to check that some information in a report is correct. What does she say?

Information	Time
Compact operated	July 1983
Compact sold products to the US	August 1985
Michael Stott worked as Production Manager	2 years
The company grown by 15% p.a.	It was set up

1. Has Compact operated since July 1983?
2. _____ Compact _____ _____ to the US _____ three years?
3. _____ _____ _____ in these premises _____ _____ _____?
4. _____ Michael Stott _____ _____ _____ _____ _____ 2 years?
5. _____ the company _____ _____ 15% p.a. _____ it was set up?

4. Transfer

■ PAIR WORK

Student B: turn to the Key section.

Student A: you are helping to train a new secretary who has joined your company. Below are the things that s/he should do in the first month. It's now the end of the first month. Check how s/he has got on and make notes, as appropriate, below.

Checklist	*Responses*
Met all the managers	Production
	Marketing
	Personnel
	Finance
Read the office rules and regulations	Yes
	Part
	No
Studied the word-processing manual	Yes
	Part
	No
Seen all the departments	Production
	Marketing
	Personnel
	Finance
Bought meal tickets for next month	Yes/no
Received details of the company sports facilities	Swimming
	Tennis
	Squash
	Aerobics
Joined any of the company clubs	Swimming
	Tennis
	Squash
	Aerobics

You should start like this:

Student A: 'Have you met all the managers yet?'
Student B: 'Well, I've only met the Production and Marketing Managers.'
Student A: 'So you haven't met the Finance and Personnel Managers yet?'
Student B: 'No, I haven't.'
Now you continue.

5. Word check

chap — familiar word for a man
pile — very large amount or number
open plan — open office area for a large number of people rather than individual small offices
boss — person who has control over others
to settle in — to get to know the place you work in

extension – addition of a new part to an existing building to make it bigger

huge – very big

temp – abbreviation for temporary – person who does a job either while the regular employee is off sick, or on holiday, or at a very busy time when additional staff are needed

Communications

(requesting and replying)

Introduction

Alice Everett has been out of the office on company business for ten days now, and Hilary Beacham, Karen Williams and Helen Wright have been very busy looking after the Marketing Department.

1a. Reading

Many of the letters to the Marketing Department are standard enquiries or requests, and there are standard replies which can be used.

Look at the following extracts from enquiry letters sent to the Marketing Department, and link the request on the left with the most appropriate reply on the right.

Request	*Reply*
1. Please could you send us a copy of your latest price list.	a. We wish to inform you that all our computers are IBM compatible.
2. We would be very grateful if you could send us details of your new accountancy packages.	b. The addresses of local stockists are given on the accompanying sheet.
3. I would be much obliged if you could let us know whether the PC-1414 is IBM compatible.	c. We are happy to enclose a copy of our latest price list.
4. I am writing to request a copy of your latest catalogue.	d. Please find enclosed a leaflet giving the details you requested.
5. We would appreciate it if you could let us know where we can buy your accountancy packages in the Manchester area.	e. We regret to inform you that our catalogue is being reprinted at present, but _____

1b. Listening 🔊

Now listen to the conversation between Hilary, Helen and Karen, in which Hilary makes a number of requests. The requests are listed on the left in the table below. On the right put a tick (✔) if Hilary receives a positive reply; put a cross (✗) if she receives a negative reply. The first one has been done for you.

Request	Reply
1. Find the file on Impex	✔
2. Make a cup of coffee	
3. Ask Alan Ford to pop in	
4. Work late tonight	
5. Work late tomorrow night	
6. Ask Karen to come in	
7. Tell her to bring the Impex file	
8. Write a quick letter	

2. Presentation

The Reading and Listening sections above presented a number of requests and replies to requests.

(a) In business letters we tend to use quite formal language, e.g.

Request
> We would be very grateful if you could ...
> I would be much obliged if you could ...
> We would appreciate if you could ...
> I am writing to request ...
> Please could you ...

Reply
> *Positive*
> Please find enclosed ...
> We are happy to enclose ...
> We wish to inform you that ...

> *Negative*
> We regret to inform you ...

(b) In speaking the form will depend on:
> our relationship with the other person;
> the nature of the request, e.g.

Request
> Can you find me the file on Impex, please?
> Could you work late tonight?
> Would you ask Alan Ford to see me, please?
> Would you mind making me a cup of coffee?

Reply
> *Positive*   *Negative*
> (After request with 'can', 'could', 'would')

Certainly, I'll do it right away.
Yes, of course.

(After request with 'would you mind')
No, of course not.

I'm afraid I . . .
I'm sorry but . . .

Well, actually . . .

3. Controlled practice

(a) Letter: requesting
Expand the following notes into appropriate requests in business letters.

1. We/grateful/you send payment/ASAP
———————————————————————

2. I/obliged/you phone/Monday a.m.
———————————————————————

3. We/appreciate/your Sales Dept. return samples
———————————————————————

4. I write/request/copy/this year price list
———————————————————————

(b) Spoken: replying
While Alice Everett has been out of the office, she has made notes on the things that need to be done when she returns. When she returns she asks Hilary Beacham to do these things. Below are Alice's requests (1–5) and Hilary's replies (a–e). Link the replies to the requests. The first one has been done for you.

Requests
1. Could you send our current price list to Brown & Partners? (c)
2. Could you give the report on the Manchester visit to the Managing Director? ( )
3. Would you mind asking Karen Williams to show me copies of the correspondence? ( )
4. Would you ask Helen Wright to file away the notes on the meeting with Collins? ( )
5. Would you mind asking Helen Wright to check the arrangements for my visit to Switzerland? ( )

Replies
a. No, of course not.
b. Well, actually they haven't been typed up yet.
c. Certainly, I'll do it right away. Should I send it by express?
d. Yes, of course. Shall I make a copy for our files?
e. I'm sorry, but she's not in today; she's ill. But I'll get them.

4. Transfer 🔘

(a) Listen to Alice Everett's dictated letter and draft it out below.

COMPACT SYSTEMS
96 Rosewall Drive, Southtown, SO3 4BT

116 Grosvenor Road
Manchester

Your ref: order number 9200CF3
Our ref: 9200CF3

17 April 19——

Dear ___ ___ ___ ___ ___

Thank ___ ___ ___ ___ ___ ___ ___ ___ ___ ___ ___ ___ ___ ___ ___
___ ___ ___ ___ ___ ___ ___ ___ ___ ___ ___ ___ ___ ___ ___ ___ ___
___ ___ ___ ___ ___ ___ ___ ___ ___ ___ ___ ___ ___ ___ ___ ___ ___
___ ___ ___ ___ ___ ___ ___ ___ ___ ___ ___ ___ ___ ___ ___ ___ ___
___ ___ ___ ___ ___ ___ ___ ___ ___ ___ ___ ___ ___ ___ ___ ___ ___
___ ___ ___ ___ ___ ___ ___.

___ ___ ___ ___ ___ ___ ___ ___ ___ ___ ___ ___.

___ ___ ___ ___ ___

___ ___ ___ ___ ___ ___
Marketing Manager

(b) You are working for a company supplying hifi equipment. Write a letter to:
  Mrs Mary White
  Witney Stereo Centre
  56 East Street
  Witney
  Oxon
In her letter to you she asked if:
  you have 12 Zanuchi stereo systems in stock;
  you can give her a 10 per cent discount;
  you can supply the equipment before the end of the month.
Your answers are:
  yes;
  yes (if account settled within 30 days);
  no (earliest delivery date 30 days after order).
Write a letter replying to her questions. (For guidance on letters of reply, see Appendix 4
— letter 3). Also ask her:
  if she requires model Z90, Z99, or Z200, and enclose details;
  if she wishes to place an order;
  to quote reference PCB023 in all correspondence.

Mrs Mary White
Witney Stereo Centre
56 East Street
Witney
Oxon

Your ref: PCB023
Our ref: PCB023/AB

17 April 19——

Dear Mrs White

Thank you for your recent letter __
__ __
__ __ __ __ __ __ __ __ __ __ __ __ __ __ __ __.

__ __
__ __
__ __ __ __ __ __ __ __ __ __ __ __ __ __.

__ __
__ __ __ __ __ __ __ __ __ __.

__ __
__ __.

Yours sincerely

__ __ __ __ __ __ __

5. Word check

right away — immediately
paperwork — written work, e.g., letters, reports, etc.
to pop in — to come in quickly for a short period of time
off sick — not at work because of illness
pile — very large amount or number

Transfer listening
to enquire — to ask
receipt — act of getting, delivery
delay — act of being late
consignment — goods sent
damaged — harmed, broken
packing — material put around a product to prevent damage during transportation
to credit — to arrange repayment either in money or in goods

Around town

(giving directions)

Introduction

Pierre Farabolini, a visitor from France, has spent three days looking round Compact. He has gone back to his hotel, the Cromarty, to collect his luggage before taking a taxi to the airport to catch the plane home.

1. Listening 🔾🔾

The phone rings in Pierre's room. Hilary has just been informed that Pierre's flight will be delayed by two hours. So Pierre decides to visit the shopping centre in Southtown. As you listen, mark the route Hilary describes on the map below, and indicate the beginning of the main shopping street.

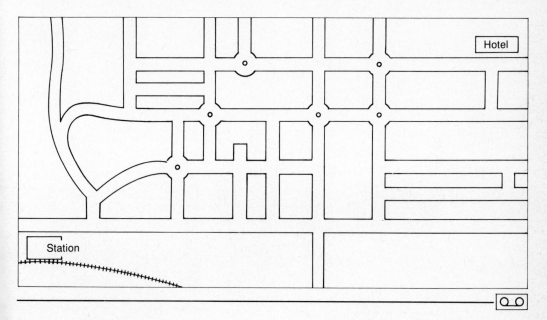

2. Presentation

Here is some of the language you have just heard. Notice how it is used to give directions.

On roads

turn left
take the first left
take the first on your left

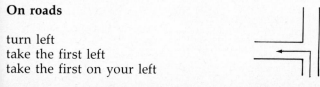

53

turn right
go right

take the second left

carry/go straight on
carry on
walk along there

At roundabouts

go left
take the first exit

go straight over
take the second exit

go right
take the third exit

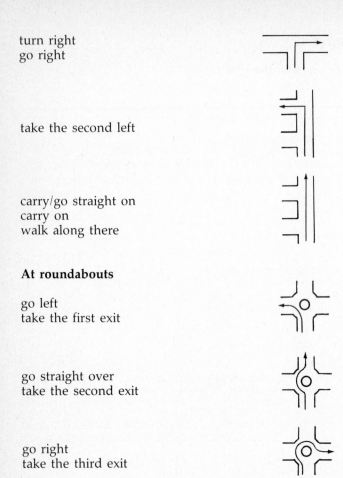

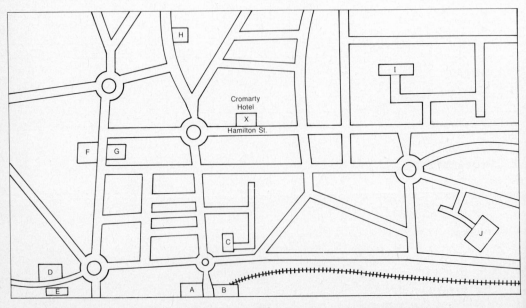

3. Controlled practice

Now look at the map below and complete the directions.

```
A = Grosvenor Hotel        E = conference centre      I = bank
B = railway station        F = Natco Ltd              J = post office
C = 19 Park Place           G = garage                 X = Cromarty Hotel
D = Charlie's restaurant    H = sports centre
```

1. From the Cromarty Hotel (X) to the bank (I).
   Turn _ _ _ _ _ out of the Cromarty Hotel and _ _ _ _ _ _ _ _ _ _. _ _ _ _ _
   left. Then turn _ _ _ _ _ and follow the road round to the right.

2. From the bank (I) to the sports centre (H).
   Go out of the bank, and follow the road round to the left. _ _ _ _ _ the _ _ _ _ _
   right, and then _ _ _ _ _ right into Hamilton Street. _ _ _ _ _ along _ _ _ _ _
   until you get to the roundabout and _ _ _ _ _ the third _ _ _ _ _. Bear _ _ _ _ _
   where the road divides and the sports centre is on your _ _ _ _ _.

3. From the sports centre (H) to Natco (F).
   _ _ _ _ _ out of the sports centre and _ _ _ _ _ the first right. At the roundabout,
   _ _ _ _ _. Natco is on your right opposite the garage.

4. From Natco (F) to the conference centre (E).
   _ _ _ _ _ out of Natco. At the roundabout take the _ _ _ _ _. The conference
   centre is on your left opposite Charlie's restaurant.

5. From the conference centre (E) to the Grosvenor Hotel (A).
   _ _ _ _ _ right out of the conference centre and _ _ _ _ _ at the roundabout. At
   the next roundabout, _ _ _ _ _ the third exit. The Grosvenor Hotel is on your right
   opposite the railway station.

6. From the Grosvenor Hotel (A) to the post office (J).
   Turn _ _ _ _ _ out of the hotel and take the _ _ _ _ _ at the roundabout. Take
   the _ _ _ _ _ left and then take the fourth _ _ _ _ _ at the roundabout. Take the
   first _ _ _ _ _ and then _ _ _ _ _ left. The post office is in front of you.

---

4. Transfer

■ PAIR WORK
Student B: turn to the Key section.

(a) **Student A:** first mark the following places on the map. You can put them in any position you choose:

    the post office;
    Western Travel Bureau;
    Maxi Supermarket;
    Westco.

You work as a secretary in a company in Southtown. Student B is a visitor to your company. He/she is staying at the Cromarty Hotel. He/she needs to get to each of the above places tomorrow in the order given. Give him/her the necessary directions from the Cromarty Hotel.

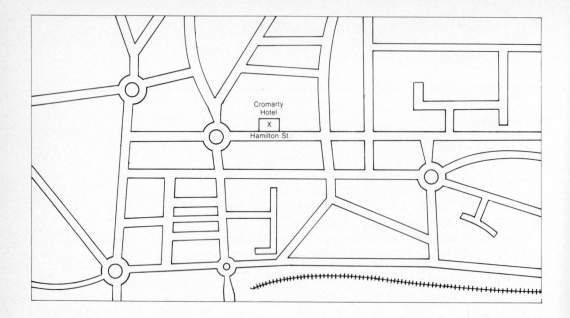

Cromarty
Hotel

X

Hamilton St.

(b) **Student A:** you are visiting a company in Southtown, and are staying at the Cromarty Hotel. You need to get to each of the following places tomorrow in the order given below:

National Bank;
the railway station;
Andy's restaurant;
Northco.

Student B is a secretary in the company you are visiting. Ask for the directions to each of the above places in the order given from the Cromarty Hotel. Indicate your route and the position of each of the places on the map.

5. Word check

luggage — suitcases or bags for carrying clothes when travelling
delayed — late
due — expected
to book — to reserve
to stretch one's legs — to have a walk, especially after sitting for a time (informal)
roundabout — circular junction of three or more roads
to hang on — to wait
junction — where two or more roads meet
don't mention it — polite reply after 'thank you'

Dissatisfied customers

(apologising)

Introduction

As Compact is not a large company, one of the functions of the Marketing Department is to sort out problems with customers. These problems are often the result of delivery delays or faulty products.

1a. Listening 🔘 ────────────────────────────────

Now that Hilary Beacham is familiar with Compact's product range, she often has to deal with the problems of dissatisfied customers and clients, although Alice Everett always asks her to make notes of any complaints. In this unit you are going to hear one complaint and read about another.

Listen to the conversation between Hilary Beacham and Paul Crown. As you listen, make notes on the form below about the reasons for Mr Crown's complaints.

```
┌─────────────────────────────────────────────────────┐
│  To: _ _ _ _ _ _ _ _                                │
│  From: _ _ _ _ _ _ _ _                              │
│                                                     │
│              While you were away                    │
│  Name: Paul Crown      Company: _____           │
│  visited:              phoned:                      │
│  returned your call:   would like a call:           │
│                                                     │
│                    Message                          │
│  Complaints:                                        │
│   1. _ _ _ _ _ _ _ _ _ _ _ _ _ _ _ _ _ _ _ _ _ _   │
│   2. _ _ _ _ _ _ _ _ _ _ _ _ _ _ _ _ _ _ _ _ _ _   │
│   3. _ _ _ _ _ _ _ _ _ _ _ _ _ _ _ _ _ _ _ _ _ _   │
└─────────────────────────────────────────────────────┘
```

── 🔘

1b. Reading

Some time later Mr Crown has another complaint about Compact. However, on this occasion he decides to put it in writing. As you read Mr Crown's letter, list the complaints on the form below.

Semantix
192 School Lane
Solihull
Birmingham

Mrs A. Everett
Compact Systems
96 Rosewall Drive
Southtown
SO3 4BT

13th July, 19——

Dear Mrs Everett

Further to our telephone conversation, I would like to point several things out to you.

Firstly, although we can accept that production difficulties at your factory have led to slight delays, we still have not received delivery of the goods due two months ago.

Secondly, your letter explaining that the consignment would be delayed arrived too late to be of any use to us.

Lastly, and most importantly, not all the units from our March order were delivered. Out of 60, we only received 58.

I would be grateful if you could phone me to give me some explanation of this.

Yours sincerely

P. Crown

P. Crown
Purchasing Manager

Complaints:
1. _____
2. _____
3. _____

2.   Presentation

On the tape Hilary Beacham apologised to Paul Crown. Here is some of the language she used:
   Routine apologies
   Sorry, could you spell that for me, please?
   I'm afraid Mrs Everett is away on business until next week.
   Stronger apologies
   I'm very/extremely sorry to hear that.
   I do apologise.
   Please accept my apologies.

To apologise in writing we use similar expressions:

We were (very/extremely/most) sorry to hear about the problem.
We regret that this problem has happened.
We apologise for the problem that has arisen.

3. Controlled practice

On the left there are a number of statements (spoken or written); on the right there are apologies. Draw lines to link the statement with its appropriate apology. The first one has been done for you.

1. My name is Crabtree	(a) I do apologise on his behalf
2. He was extremely rude	(b) Please accept my apologies
3. Four items were damaged	(c) Sorry, could you repeat that, please?
4. The delivery was late	(d) I'm afraid she's not available at the moment
5. Your rep did not call	(e) I do apologise for his behaviour
6. Mrs Blythe, please	(f) I am extremely sorry for the error made by our accounts department
7. We were surprised to receive an invoice as the goods have been returned	(g) We are sorry about the damaged items
8. Your cheque has been returned to us by our bank	(h) We regret the delay, but it is due to circumstances beyond our control

4. Transfer

(a) Speaking
Before starting this activity, look at the telephone language in Appendix 1.

■ PAIR WORK
Student B: turn to the Key section.
Student A: you are Paul Crown. Look again at your letter of complaint above. You are going to receive a phone call from Student B (Hilary Beacham). During the call, complete your notes below:

Complaint	Compact's finding	Agreed action
Late delivery of May order Late arrival of letter of explanation Two missing items from March order		

When you answer the phone, remember to:
  introduce yourself;
  thank your caller for her prompt call;
  acknowledge the action on each complaint;
  express satisfaction/dissatisfaction with the offer/action;

summarise the main points of the call;
ask for a written confirmation;
end the call.

(b) Writing
Based on the phone conversation you have just had, write a letter of apology to Mr Crown confirming the details you discussed. Before doing this activity you may wish to refer to the model letters in Appendix 4.

COMPACT SYSTEMS
96 Rosewall Drive, Southtown, SO3 4BT

Mr P. Crown
Semantix
192 School Lane
Solihull
Birmingham

17th July, 19——

Dear Mr Crown

Further to my phone call earlier today, I should like to apologise again for the unfortunate events and to confirm the details of our conversation. As I explained, Mrs Everett is abroad; therefore I investigated your complaints.

Firstly, we are __
order. I can assure you that __ __ __ __ __ __ __ __ __ __ __ __ __ __ __ and will reach
__ __ __ __ __ __. Because of the inconvenience __ __ __ __ __ __ __ __ __ __ __ __ __ __
discount.

Secondly, __
__ __
__ __ __ __ __ arrived late. This was unfortunately __ __ __ __ __ __ __ __ __ __ __.

Lastly, I __
missing. Unfortunately __ __ __ __ __ __ __ __ __ __ __ __ __ __ __ __ __ __ __ 60. The two
remaining items __ __ __ __ __ today.

I should like to assure you that __ __ __ __ __ __ __ __ __ __ __ __ __ __ __.

__ __ __ __ __ __

H. Beacham
Personal Assistant to Alice Everett

Your letter should include the following details:
    the correspondent's name and address;
    the date;
    a greeting;
    apology for unfortunate events;
    confirmation of phone conversation;
    Mrs Everett is abroad – therefore you investigated the complaints;

complaints, findings and actions (above);
assurance that this will not happen again;
final greeting.

5. Word check

link up − co-operation
product range − different products produced by a company
rep − abbreviation for representative (see representative)
to turn up − to arrive
annoyed − angry
misunderstanding − failure to do something as a result of poor communications
rude − impolite
appropriate − suitable
to show up − to arrive
to get back − to call back

UNIT 16 **Work routines**

(expressions of frequency)

Introduction

There's a little disagreement in the office about work routines. Two of the secretaries, Karen and Helen, are complaining to Hilary about the amount of extra work they have to do.

1. Listening 🔘

As you listen, fill in the details about the frequency of their office routines in the table below. The first one has been done for you.

	Karen	Helen
sort through the post take minutes at board meetings take dictation type up minutes type letters distribute mail	——— often	

2. Presentation

Here is some of the language you have just heard. Notice how it is used to express definite and indefinite frequency.

(a) Definite frequency

once
twice
three times   an hour/a day/a week/a month/a year
four times, etc.

every day/week /month /year
daily   /weekly/monthly/yearly
                    /annually

every three months = quarterly

e.g. Well, I do that twice a day ...
    Well, I take minutes at the board meeting every month ...

(b) Indefinite frequency

most frequent

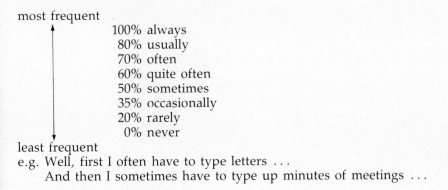

        100% always
        80% usually
        70% often
        60% quite often
        50% sometimes
        35% occasionally
        20% rarely
        0% never

least frequent
e.g. Well, first I often have to type letters ...
    And then I sometimes have to type up minutes of meetings ...

3. Controlled practice

(a) Definite frequency

The notes below show how often things are done in the company. Use the information to complete the sentences with expressions of definite frequency. The first one has been done for you.

---

1. Postal collection: 10.30, 14.00, 15.00
   The post is collected three times a day
2. Post delivery: 8.30, 13.00
   The post is delivered _____ _____ _____.
3. Photocopier service: January, April, July, October
   The photocopier is serviced _____ _____ _____.
4. Canteen tickets for sale: Mondays
   Canteen tickets are sold _____ _____ _____.
5. Telephone check: March
   The telephones are checked _____.
6. Fire alarm test: June, December
   The fire alarms are tested _____ _____ _____.
7. New staff training courses: January, February, March, etc.
   Training courses for new staff are held _____ _____.

(b) Indefinite frequency

Here are the results of a survey carried out into the activities of Compact employees. Use the information and the expressions of indefinite frequency in the Presentation to write sentences about Compact employees. The first one has been done for you.

1. Read the company newsletter	35%
2. Look at the notice boards	20%
3. Eat in the company canteen	60%
4. Work overtime	50%
5. Take their full holiday entitlement	100%
6. Come to work by car	80%
7. Retire at 65	70%
8. Are made redundant	0%

1. Compact employees occasionally read the company newsletter.
2. _____
3. _____
4. _____
5. _____
6. _____
7. _____
8. _____

4. Transfer

■ GROUP WORK

For this activity work in groups of four. Below are some of the work routines that Helen and Karen had to do. Are your work routines similar? What other work routines do you have? How often do you have to do them? Discuss with the other members of your group.

Work routines
Sort through the post
Take minutes at board meetings
Take dictation
Type up minutes
Type letters
Distribute mail

5. Word check

to manage to − to be able to
minutes − record of things that were said and decided in a meeting
to sort through − to put into order
to distribute − to divide among several or many people
dictation − act of writing down what is said (e.g., a letter from a boss)
board meeting − meeting of the directors of a company

UNIT 17 The suggestions box

(making suggestions)

Introduction

In the Marketing Department there is a 'suggestions box' into which the staff from the department are encouraged to put their suggestions for improving efficiency. It is one of Hilary Beacham's jobs to check the box and to report to Alice Everett. Today Hilary has decided to look at the suggestions that have been made during the last month.

1a. Reading

Read the following suggestion extracts and then organise them into their appropriate box below:
  equipment
  working procedures
  general

---

1. I suggest that we change the time of the morning tea break so that it starts at 10.30 rather than 11.00.

2. I recommend that we replace the printer as soon as possible, as it is very noisy.

3. I really think we should have a non-smoking office. In other companies . . .

4. I advise the company to introduce flexitime before they lose more of their staff. Most of the other companies in Southtown already . . .

5. I suggest that we organise a company Christmas party. It would be . . .

6. Now that you've had a chance to settle in, I recommend that you do something about reorganising the furniture in this office. I think it's . . .

equipment	working procedures	general

1b. Listening 🔊

Now listen to the conversation between Hilary and Alice. As you listen, indicate in the appropriate column if Alice agrees or disagrees with the suggestion.

Suggestion	Agrees	Disagrees
1. tea break at 10.30		
2. new printer		
3. non-smoking office		
4. flexitime		
5. company Christmas party		
6. reorganising the furniture		

2. Presentation

Now let's look at some of the language used to make suggestions. We can divide it into written suggestions and spoken suggestions.

Written suggestions
The following verbs are used for formal written suggestions:
advise
suggest
recommend
e.g. I advise the company to introduce flexitime.
    I suggest (that) we organise a company Christmas party.
    I recommend that we replace the printer as soon as possible.

Spoken suggestions
In speech we use the following constructions:
I think we should have it a bit earlier.
It might be a good idea to fit a better cover.
What about having a non-smoking office?
Why don't you talk informally to the office staff?
Don't you think we should consider it?

3. Controlled practice

Complete the following sentences with the most appropriate choice, a, b, or c.

1. _ _ _ _ _ buy some new office furniture.
   (a) I think we
   (b) I think we should
   (c) I think we should to

2. _ _ _ _ _ organise a leaving party for Mr Brown.
   (a) I suggest that we
   (b) I suggest to
   (c) I suggest us to

3. _ _ _ _ _ buy him a present.
   (a) It might be a good idea
   (b) It might be a good idea if
   (c) It might be a good idea to

4. _ _ _ _ _ organise some drinks for the party?
   (a) Why don't you
   (b) How about to
   (c) Why don't you to

5. _ _ _ _ _ think about this matter carefully.
   (a) I advise to
   (b) I advise you to
   (c) I advise to you to

6. _ _ _ _ _ Mrs Brown?
   (a) What about to invite
   (b) What about invite
   (c) What about inviting

7. _ _ _ _ _ his whole family?
   (a) Don't you think we should to invite
   (b) Don't you think we should invite
   (c) Don't you think we invite

8. _ _ _ _ _ make this company policy.
   (a) I recommend to
   (b) I recommend that we
   (c) I recommend us to

4. Transfer

■ GROUP WORK

Discuss these problems and make suggestions as to how they might be solved.

(a) A memo has arrived at your office from the Managing Director. He says that there is £6,000 available for office improvements. In your group, draw up a list of six possible improvements.

(b) The annual staff outing is approaching. The Office Manager needs some suggestions for things you would like to do (places to visit, etc.). Draw up a list of six suggestions.

5. Word check

to improve – to make better
efficiency – ability to work well
to have no objections – to agree
cover – top of piece of equipment
to investigate – to look in detail into something
flexitime – system of flexible working hours
all in favour – in total agreement
cramped – limited in space

The board meeting

(present perfect v. past simple)

Introduction

Compact Systems have a number of regular meetings during the year. The most important is the annual Board Meeting, at which the company's performance over the year is presented and discussed.

1. Listening 🔘

Mary Wilkins, the Managing Director's Personal Assistant, has been asked to take notes at the Board Meeting. In this section David Burton, the Managing Director, presents statistics on the company's growth. Listen to them discussing Compact Systems' performance, and complete the table below.

	UK	Spain	W. Germany	France
1985				
1986				
1987				
1988				

2. Presentation

Here is some of the language you have just heard. Notice how the present perfect and the past simple are used differently.

PAST TENSE
(i) The past tense is used to refer to something that happened at a particular point of time (X) in the past. For example:

> I arrived on Monday. PAST $- - - X - - $ NOW $- - - - - - -$ FUTURE
> He started last year. $- X - - - - -$ NOW $- - - - - - -$

(ii) It is also used to refer to a period of time (X $- - - $ X) in the past:

> I spent two weeks in Germany. PAST $- X - X - - $ NOW $- - - - $ FUTURE
> I worked on it for two days. $- X - X - - $ NOW $- - - - $

PRESENT PERFECT
(i) The present perfect is used to refer to an action which started at a definite point of time in the past and continues to the present (X $- - - $ NOW).

This period of time may be:

(a) understood from the context —

Allan Ford has performed very well.
PAST — — — X — — — NOW — — — — — — — FUTURE
i.e., in the time since he joined the company.

(b) stated in the text —

We've made good progress there between 1985 and now.
PAST — — — X — — — NOW — — — — — — — FUTURE

(ii) The present perfect is also used to refer to an action which started at an indefinite point of time in the past, but which has a result in the present (X — — — NOW).

Two other UK firms in our market have branched out into Spain.
PAST — — — X — — — NOW — — — — — — — FUTURE
Present result: increased competition

(iii) The present perfect is also used after 'just' and 'recently' to indicate an action in the very recent past, which is almost considered part of the present (X NOW).

I've literally just arrived back.
PAST — — — — — X — NOW — — — — — — — FUTURE

3. Controlled practice

Circle the correct verb from the choice given to complete the following statement made in a meeting. The first one has been done for you.

So, you have heard/heard the highlights of our activities last year and the main details of our market plan for next year. In conclusion I would like to say that last year we have made/made a good profit from our activities in South America. As a result we have consolidated/consolidated our market position. In November I have visited/visited our subsidiary in Portugal, and I was/have been very pleased with our staff out there. They have worked/worked very hard to establish our products in the market. Mr Suares, the General Manager, showed/has shown me round the plant, and it was/has been a very interesting experience. He has been/was in charge for nearly one year now and he has improved/improved efficiency enormously. In fact I just received/have just received a note from him, and it seems that last month sales increased/have increased by another 12 per cent. So, things are looking good.

4. Transfer

You have been asked by your boss (Mr Barry) to draft a letter giving an account of a meeting that happened last week. For further guidance, see Appendix 4, p. 171.
   Write a letter to:
   Mr R.V. White
   103 Spalding Road
   Chiswick
   London.

Include the following things in your letter —

PAST TENSE:
   10.30 meeting open + minutes approved;
   1.00 lunch;
   2.30 tour of factory;
   4.00 reception at nearby hotel;
   6.00 dinner at hotel;
   9.00 representatives return to hotels.

PRESENT PERFECT:
   South American market has improved;
   South American profits have increased.

   Mr Barry has asked about the report from Mr White on the African market. Has he sent it?

Mr R.V. White
103 Spalding Road
Chiswick
London

15 August 19——

Dear Mr White

I have been asked to write to you giving an account of last week's meeting.

The meeting began at __.

Now for some details about the South American market. __.

Finally, Mr Barry has asked about __?

__ __ __ __ __ __ __ __ __ __ __ __.

__ __ __ __ __ __

5. Word check

slight − very small or short
item − point
agenda − list of things to be discussed in a meeting
annual − every year
to copy − to make something the same as another thing
to perform − to do a job
commendable − worthy of praise
specifics − not general information
turning point − significant event for a company (usually positive)
to branch out − to add to the range of one's activities
(marketing) drive − special effort
representative − person who visits clients to present his/her company's products or services
domestic (market) − home

Considering job applicants

(telephoning 2)

Introduction

Compact is looking forward to a successful year. They expect orders to increase and therefore the company has decided to recruit a new secretary for the Marketing Department.

1a. Reading

As you read through Compact's advertisement, indicate the requirements in the table below.

COMPACT SYSTEMS

Secretary

required to assist in busy Marketing Department. If you have experience of working in a computer company, have good typing and shorthand, and have a pleasant telephone manner, then we have the job for you. For an initial discussion, phone Hilary Beacham on 0927-423845.

---

1. _____
2. _____
3. _____

1b. Listening

Now listen to extracts from two phone calls from a prospective applicant. As you listen, choose the most appropriate message.

Call 1

Message

Date: 19 July 19——   Time: 10.30
For: Hilary Beacham
Miss Adel Right phoned. Please call her after 14.00.   (1)

Message

Date: 19 July 19——   Time: 11.00
For: Hilary Beacham
Mrs Adel Wright phoned. Please call her after 14.00.   (2)

```
                          Message

    Date: 19 July 19——   Time: 11.30
    For: Hilary Beacham
    Mrs Adel Wright phoned. She'll call you after 14.00.        (3)
```

```
                          Message

    Date: 19 July 19——      Time: 13.30
    For: Hilary Beacham
    Mrs Adel Wright phoned. She'll call you after 14.00.        (4)
```

Call 2

```
                     Notes on Applicants

    Name: Miss Adel Wright
    Details: 4 years – BD Systems – marketing department
             Handles written and phone enquiries
             Doesn't do a lot of typing
             Rusty shorthand                                    (1)
```

```
                     Notes on Applicants

    Name: Mrs Adel Wright
    Details: 4 years – DB Systems – sales department
             Handles written and phone enquiries
             Doesn't do a lot of typing
             Rusty shorthand                                    (2)
```

```
                     Notes on Applicants

    Name: Mrs Adel Wright
    Details: 4 years – DB Systems – sales department
             Handles written and phone enquiries
             Does a lot of typing
             Rusty shorthand                                    (3)
```

2. Presentation

Let's consider the phone calls made by Adel Wright in terms of the language she needed to understand. Look at the following steps in the phone conversation between the switchboard and Hilary Beacham:

identifying one's company and oneself;
asking for the caller's identification;
asking for further information;
connecting the caller;
explaining that someone is not available;
alternative actions.

Now let's look at the language used for these steps:

1. Identifying the company:
   Compact Systems.
2. Identifying oneself:
   Hilary Beacham speaking.
3. Asking for the caller's identification:
   Who's calling, please?
   And your name is?
4. Asking for further information:
   And what's it in connection with, please?
   And what's it about, please?
5. Connecting the caller:
   One moment, please.
   Hold on a moment, please.
   I'm putting you through now.
   I'll just connect you.
6. Explaining that someone is not available:
   I'm afraid there's no answer.
7. Alternative actions:
   Would you like to leave a message?
   If you give me your name, I'll tell her you ...

Note:
When you identify yourself as the caller, you use one of the following expressions:
   My name is _ _ _ _ _ _.
   This is _ _ _ _ _ _ here.
   Hilary Beacham, here.
When you identify yourself as the called person, you use one of the following expressions:
   Hilary Beacham speaking.
   Hilary Beacham.

3. Controlled practice

Choose the most appropriate response from the alternatives given.

---

1. (*Ring, ring*)
   (a) This is Hilary Beacham.
   (b) Hilary Beacham speaking.
   (c) I am Hilary Beacham.

2. Can I speak to Paul Jordan, please?
   (a) Who's calling, please?
   (b) What's your name?
   (c) I am.

3. My name's Hilary Beacham.
   (a) What's it with, please?
   (b) What's it for, please?
   (c) What's it about, please?

4. Next month's sales conference.
   (a) Hold on a moment, please.
   (b) Wait.
   (c) Don't go away.

5. (*Ring, ring*)
   (a) I'm afraid he isn't.
   (b) I'm afraid there's no answer.
   (c) I'm afraid he doesn't answer.

6. Would you like to leave a message?
   (a) Please tell him to give me a phone.
   (b) Please tell him to give me a call.
   (c) Please tell him to give me a ring.

---

4. Transfer

Before starting this activity refer to Appendix 1 — Telephone language (p. 166).

■ PAIR WORK

Student B: turn to the Key section.

Student A: you work as PA/Secretary to the Marketing Manager. Your boss, Mr Marks, is on a sales trip to the USA at the moment. You have just received the following fax from one of your UK suppliers:

From: Frederick Delsey
To: John Marks

Please call me today. A matter of great urgency has arisen. I will be contactable at the following numbers at the following UK local times:

09.00−12.00	01-324 6785
12.00−15.00	01-324 9872
15.00−18.00	01-576 0945
18.00−23.00	01-324 8923

Your boss has left you the following rough schedule of his movements for today.
    ABT – meeting from 8.00–11.00 with Joe Rondule.
    Nova – possible new supplier – meeting before lunch (?).
    Lunch with Tony Armstrong of Supra.
    15.00 – call Jerry Abram to fix meeting.
    16.00 – fly to Detroit – City hotel.

You decide to phone the organisations in the following order:
    ABT (switchboard and PA/secretary to Joe Rondule);
    Nova (switchboard and PA/secretary to Sales Manager);
    Supra (switchboard and PA/secretary to Tony Armstrong);
    City hotel in Detroit (receptionist).

Remember to:
    identify yourself;
    explain the purpose of your call;
    leave a message where appropriate;
    thank your correspondent for his/her help.

5. Word check

in connection with – about
paper – newspaper
duty – something you must do
to handle – to deal with, organise
enquiry – question
rusty – forgotten because not used

UNIT 20 **Organising the typing pool**

(cause and effect)

Introduction

Compact has recently recruited a new secretary called Jo Cooper to join the Production Department. Because of the addition of a new secretary, there will obviously be an effect on the work of the department.

1a. Reading

After Jo was appointed, Christine Adams, the Office Manager, sent a memo round the departmental heads at Compact. While you are reading the memo, indicate in the appropriate column the causes and effects mentioned in it. The first one has been done for you.

MEMO

15 September 19——

To: Departmental heads
From: Christine Adams
     Office Manager

Owing to the recent increase in business, we have a backlog of work in the Production Department. This, in turn, has led to problems in other departments. Because we expect business to increase still further, we have appointed a new secretary for production. On the one hand the addition of a new secretary will certainly improve efficiency; on the other hand this appointment may now result in backlogs in other departments. We shall have to see.

Causes	Effects
1. increase in business	backlog of work in the production department
2.	
3.	
4.	
5.	

1b. Listening 🔊

Now listen to the tape of Christine discussing her plans with Jane Williams and Samantha Wolf, the present secretaries in the Production Department. In the conversation you will hear the causes and effects of these plans. As you listen, write a 'C' for cause or an 'E' for effect in the table below. The first one has been done for you.

Jo is going to start on Monday (C)	Jane's and Samantha's responsibilities will be affected (E)
Jo Cooper is new	Jane will show her round
Jo will visit the main departments	It's important that she gets an idea of the company's activities
Taking newcomers around the departments	a bit of trouble
backlog of work	things are a bit chaotic
Jane will be busy with Jo	Samantha will look after the phone
Samantha will look after the phone	she won't have time to deal with all the correspondence
backlog of work	the great number of phone calls
great number of phone calls	Jo will start looking after the phone
Jane can concentrate on the correspondence and paperwork	she won't have to worry about the phone

---

| Q O |

2. Presentation

In the memo and the conversation, there were a number of expressions indicating cause and effect.
   These can be divided into:
   verbs of cause and effect;
   conjunctions of cause;
   adverb phrases of cause;
   adverbial links.

Now let's look at these in greater detail.

(a) Verbs of cause and effect; these include:
      to lead to
      to cause
      to result in
e.g. This, in turn, has led to problems in other departments.

(b) Conjunctions of cause: a conjunction links two parts of a sentence together. Conjunctions of cause include:
      because
      as
      since
e.g. Because Jo is new to the company, I would like you to spend Monday and Tuesday showing her around.

(c) Adverb phrases of cause – these introduce the cause and include:
      due to
      because of
      owing to
These phrases must be followed by a noun (phrase),
e.g. Owing to the recent increase in business, we have a backlog of work in the production department.

(d) Adverbial links: here we are focusing on a cause in a previous sentence. Adverbial links include:

therefore
so
that's why (informal)
e.g. On Monday and Tuesday Jane will be busy with Jo. So, I'd like you to look after the phone.

3. Controlled practice

Now look at the following pairs of linked events.
(a) First indicate which are causes (C) and which effects (E). The first one has been done for you.
1. I forgot to set the alarm clock. (C)
   I didn't wake up in time. (E)
2. I missed the bus.
   I didn't wake up in time.
3. I missed the bus.
   I arrived late at work.
4. My boss was very angry.
   I arrived late at work.
5. My boss shouted at me.
   My boss was very angry.
6. I shouted at my boss.
   My boss shouted at me.
7. My boss sacked me.
   I shouted at my boss.
8. I am unemployed.
   I forgot to set the alarm clock.

(b) Now complete the text based on the notes above by using a suitable expression of cause and effect.

Last Monday I forgot to set the alarm clock. _____ I didn't wake up in time. _____
I didn't wake up in time, I missed the bus. _____ of this, I arrived late at work. _____
my boss was very angry. _____ he was very angry, he shouted at me. _____ I
shouted at him. Unfortunately this shouting _____ to the sack. So now I am unemployed
_____ I forgot to set my alarm clock.

4. Transfer

Think of a series of linked events as in the Controlled practice exercise.
(a) Write notes on the series of linked events in the flowchart boxes below.
(b) Tell your partner about the events, using as many different cause and effect expressions. Your partner should write down the details in the boxes below.
Then reverse roles.

Flowchart boxes for Student A.

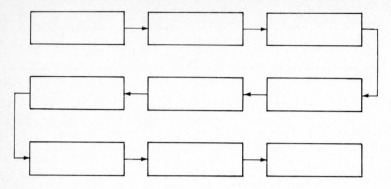

Flowchart boxes for Student B.

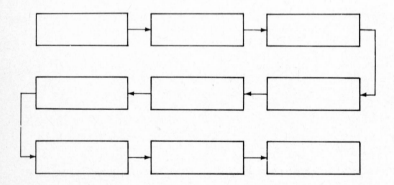

5. Word check

backlog (of work) — a lot of work which needs to be done
to appoint — to employ
efficiency — ability to work well
responsibility — what you must do
activities — different jobs done in a company
newcomer — somebody who is new
to warn — to tell in advance
buzz — phone call (informal)
procedure — way of doing something
chaotic — very busy
correspondence — letters
to catch up — to get up to date (by clearing the backlog)
to concentrate — to keep all one's attention on one subject
to solve — to find an answer to a problem
to handle — to manage
to reckon — to think

Preparing the agenda

(sequencing)

Introduction

Hilary Beacham is working with Alice Everett on the preparation of the final agenda for a meeting the following week.

1a. Reading

Alice has made some notes for items to be included on the agenda as follows:

> *Investment in new equipment*
> *New product range*
> *Review of market research activities. Staffing of marketing department.*
> *Communication*
> *Backlog of orders*
> *Workers' Council*
> *Pay reviews*

1b. Listening 📼 ───────────────────────────

Now listen to the tape and as you listen, fill in the details of the items to be included on the agenda for the meeting.

> Day/date:
> Time:
> Distribution:
>
>   *Agenda*
>
> 1.
> 2.
> 3.
> 4.
> 5.
> 6.
> 7.

2. Presentation

Here is some of the language you have just heard. Notice how it is used to express the sequence of items and events.

BEGINNING
First(ly) ...
To start with ...
Initially ...
e.g. To start with we need a date for the meeting.
    Initially I thought Tuesday 11th September.

LATER STAGES
Second(ly) ...
Third(ly) ...
Fourth(ly) ...
Then ...
Once we've discussed that, we'll go on to consider ...
Next ...
e.g. then I've received some suggestions from the other managers.
    So put that down as the second point.
    And thirdly?
    Next we'll get onto the forthcoming advertising campaign.

ENDING
Final(ly) ...
Last(ly) ...
The last thing is ...
That just leaves ...
e.g. what's the last thing on the agenda?
    that just leaves 'Computerisation of the market research programme' as my final point for the agenda.
    So, finally we've got 'Computerisation of the market research programme'.

Notice the difference in use between adjective form (without —ly) and the adverb form (with —ly).
(a) We can use either the adjective or the adverb form of ordinal numbers (first, second, third, etc.) and of 'last' to indicate the number of the step,
    e.g. first(ly) I'll present the European marketing effort
(b) We use the adverb form 'initially' and 'finally' to indicate the first and last step,
    e.g. finally we've got 'Computerisation ...'
(c) We use the adjective form when the ordinal number stands before a noun,
    e.g. so put that down as the second point
(d) After the verbs 'put' and 'take' we use the adjective forms,
    e.g. put 'review of market research activities' third.
        We'll take the advertising campaign fourth.

3. Controlled practice

Look at these agendas for meetings. As the chairperson it is your job to introduce the order of points on the agenda. Complete the texts with information from the agendas and appropriate sequence words or expressions.

Marketing meeting
1. Minutes of last meeting
2. Marketing reports: France and Germany
3. Marketing reports: Spain and Italy
4. Programme for next year
5. Date of next meeting

Before we start the meeting I'd like to go over the order of business, as there will be a small change. To _____ _____ we are going to hear the minutes of the _____ _____. Once we _____ _____ the minutes, we are going to move on to the _____ point. However, we are going to leave the _____ point on your agendas till later in the meeting. That means the _____ item will be the programme _____ _____ _____. _____ we are going to consider the _____ point on your agendas – the Marketing reports for Spain and Italy. _____ we are going to set _____ _____ _____ _____ _____ _____.

Office meeting
1. Changes in work schedules
2. 'No smoking' arrangements
3. Holiday arrangements
4. Next year's pay rise
5. Arrangements for sick leave
6. General discussion

I have decided to change the order of the items on the agenda. Because I feel that pay increases are uppermost in your minds, we will take that _____. _____, because of the problems we have had with illness I'd like to take arrangements for sick leave _____. Then I'd like to return to the beginning, to the _____ point – changes _____ _____ _____. That leaves us with the _____ point – _____ _____ _____. And _____ we will have _____ _____ _____.

---

4. Transfer

■ GROUP WORK
Here is the agenda for a meeting you are going to hold.

Agenda

1. Frequency of use of English in your office
2. Tasks/activities for which English used
3. Problems of English use
4. Suggested solutions

One of you should act as chairperson to introduce the agenda, and control the meeting. The others should act as participants in the meeting to discuss the items on the agenda.

The chairperson should start as follows:

Before we start the meeting I'd like to go over the order of business. The items on the agenda are:
1. _ _ _ _ _
2. _ _ _ _ _
3. _ _ _ _ _
4. _ _ _ _ _

If everyone agrees with the order of the points, let's start with point one . . ., could you tell us how often English is used in your office?

---

5. Word check

agenda − list of points to be discussed in a meeting
available − free
to attend − to be there
distribution list − list of people who should receive a document
forthcoming − happening in the near future
campaign − connected set of actions intended to obtain a particular business result (e.g. advertising campaign)
review − careful consideration
market research − gathering of market information especially before designing a new product
computerisation − introduction of computers into a company or department
investment − spending money on new equipment
AOB − abbreviation for 'Any Other Business'

Arranging deliveries to/from the factory

(passive verb forms)

Introduction

Helen Wright is one of the secretaries in Compact. She has been asked to make three phone calls:
  two to chase up the delivery of goods which have been ordered by Compact;
  one to arrange the delivery of Compact goods to another company.

1. Listening 🔘

Whenever one of the secretaries at Compact makes or receives a phone call about goods ordered or goods to be delivered she has to fill in a phone message slip. As you listen to the three telephone calls, fill in the phone message slips for Helen.

Phone Message Slip

Company: Expo Packaging   Called: Was called: ✔
Goods:
Order number:
Quantity:
Delivery date:
Time:
Message taken by: Helen Wright
Date: 6 January   Time: 9.45

Phone Message Slip

Company: *Zenith*   Called: Was called:
Goods:
Order number:
Quantity:
Delivery date:
Time:
Message taken by:
Date: 6 January   Time: 10.30

```
                      Phone Message Slip

     Company:                    Called:      Was called:
     Goods:
     Order number:
     Quantity:
     Delivery date:
     Time:
     Message taken by:
     Date: 6 January    Time: 15.20
```

2. Presentation

In the phone calls the speakers used a number of passive verb forms. We use the passive when we are more interested in the OBJECT (the boxes, the order, etc.) than the SUBJECT (the suppliers).

The present, past, and present perfect forms are formed from the verb 'to be' + the past participle, e.g.

the boxes are needed before then;
they were ordered about a week ago;
the purchasing officer has just been called to the factory.

Other forms of the passive (i.e. after 'will' or modal verbs) are formed from 'will' (or the modal) + 'be' + the past participle, e.g.

when our order will be delivered;
our order has to be delivered before next week.

3. Controlled practice

Below are some phone message slips. Expand the information and messages on the slips using passive forms. The first one has been done for you.

```
                      Phone Message Slip

     Company: Fisher
     Goods: 100 PCBs
     Delivery date: next Friday
     Time: morning
     Message: delivery by van
```

(a) 100 PCBs will be delivered next Friday morning by van.

```
                    Phone Message Slip

        Company: Astral
        Goods: Hot plate for canteen
        Delivery date: maybe in 2 weeks
        Message: ordered from manufacturer one week ago.
```

(b) The hot plate for the canteen, which _____ _____ from the manufacturer one week ago, _____ _____ _____ in 2 weeks.

```
                    Phone Message Slip

        Company: Office Supplies
        Goods: Filing cabinet
        Delivery date: today
        Time: afternoon
        Message: loaded on van this morning
```

(c) The filing cabinet _____ _____ on the van this morning and _____ _____ _____ this afternoon.

```
                    Phone Message Slip

        Company: Supersoft
        Goods: 50 printers
        Order date: last Tuesday
        Delivery date: next Thursday
        Time: morning
        Message: urgently needed; Compact must deliver on time
```

(d) Fifty printers _____ _____ last Tuesday. They _____ urgently _____ and _____ _____ _____ on time next Thursday morning.

4. Transfer

(a) Speaking
Before starting this exercise refer to the telephone language in Appendix 1, p. 166.

■ PAIR WORK
Student B: turn to the Key section.

Student A: you work as PA/Secretary to Bernard Wallis, Managing Director of Carnage Shipping Ltd in the UK. You have received an order for three computers from Barry Okunwe, Managing Director of Niger Sea Transport in Lagos, Nigeria. Your boss has asked you to phone Mr Okunwe to inform him of the present situation.

Phone Mr Okunwe using the following information:
Order reference: B456/C;
Goods: 3 computers;
Order placed: 14 July;
Expected delivery: late October;
Payment: invoice enclosed in letter of confirmation;
Action for Okunwe: (i) his signature required to accept delivery conditions (document enclosed) and (ii) return of document to us.

(b) Writing
Complete the following letters from the details and notes below. Before you do this activity, refer to the model letters in Appendix 4, p. 171.
(i) Now confirm the details of the phone call with Niger Sea Transport, using the following notes.

From: B. Wallis, Managing Director, Carnage Shipping Ltd, The Wharf, Southampton, England.

To: B. Okunwe, Managing Director, Niger Sea Transport, Lagos, Nigeria.

Order: B456/C
Goods: 3 computers
Order placed: 14 July
Delivery: late October
Payment: invoice enclosed
Special conditions: 1. signature to accept delivery conditions required; 2. return of document to us

Carnage Shipping Ltd
The Wharf
Southampton
England

_ _ _ _ _ _ _ _ _ _ _
_ _ _ _ _ _ _ _ _ _ _
_ _ _ _ _ _ _ _ _ _ _
_ _ _ _ _ _ _ _ _ _ _
_ _ _ _ _ _ _ _ _ _ _

_ _ _ _ _ _ _ _ _ _

Dear Mr _____

re: _ _ _ _ _ _ _ _ _ _ _ _ _ _ _

I should like to confirm the details of my phone call with your office today in connection with your order for three computers which _ _ _ _ _ _ _ _ _ _ _ on 14 July. We expect that these _ _ _ _ _ _ _ _ _ _ at the end of October. Our invoice _ _ _ _ _ _ _ _ _ _ _ _ _.

Your signature on the delivery conditions document _ _ _ _ _ _ _ _ _ _ _ _ _ _.
Therefore, I would be much obliged if this document could _ _ _ _ _ _ _ _ _ _ _ by you and _ _ _ _ _ _ _ _ _ _ to us as soon as possible.

_ _ _ _ _ _ _ _ _

_ _ _ _ _ _ _ _ _

_ _ _ _ _ _ _ _ _

(ii) Write the reply letter to Carnage Shipping Ltd using the following notes.

To: B. Wallis, Managing Director, Carnage Shipping Ltd, The Wharf, Southampton, England.

From: B. Okunwe, Managing Director, Niger Sea Transport, Lagos, Nigeria.

Order: B456/C
Thank you for letter/give date
Accept delivery conditions/document signed and enclosed
State that you will make payment as soon as the goods received
Say that you will need two more computers early next year/discuss these on next
   visit to UK

                                   Niger Sea Transport
                                      Lagos
Mr B. Wallis   Nigeria
Managing Director
Carnage Shipping Ltd
The Wharf
Southampton
England

25 August 19____

Dear Mr Wallis

re: Order B456/C

Thank you __
__ __
__ __
__ __
__ __
__ __ __ __ __ __ __ __ __ __ __ __ __ __.

In addition, __
__ __
__ __
__ __
__ __ __ __ __ __ __ __ __ __ __.

Yours sincerely

B Okunwe
Managing Director

---

5. Word check

to chase up − to get something more quickly
to connect − to join by phone
to drop off − to deliver
Purchasing (Department) − buying
consignment − goods to be delivered

Office equipment selection

(dimension and size)

Introduction

Christine Adams has now discussed with all the office staff the office equipment which is needed by the various departments. She has prepared a list, and just has to make a final check that the items she has selected will fit into the space available.

1. Listening 〔oͦo〕 ——————————————————————————

Christine Adams and Helen Wright are looking at the list of equipment to be bought for the main office, where Helen works. Christine has asked Helen to check that the dimensions of each piece of equipment are suitable. As you listen to their discussion, fill in the specifications of each item in the table below.

	Height	Length	Width	Depth
Filing cabinet Printer Word processor Desk Partition				

〔oͦo〕

2. Presentation

Now look at the diagrams below. Notice how the expressions are used to describe dimensions and size.

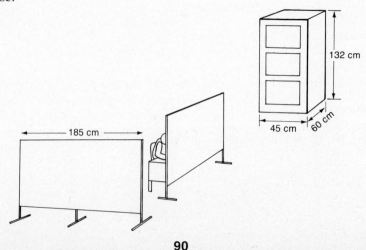

185 cm

132 cm

45 cm   60 cm

Dimensions and size

132 cm high	132 cm in height	the height of the cabinet is 132 cm
45 cm wide	45 cm in width	the width of the cabinet is 45 cm
60 cm deep	60 cm in depth	the depth of the cabinet is 60 cm
185 cm long	185 cm in length	the length of the partition is 185 cm

Notice the following questions about dimensions:
How long is the partition?
What's the length of the partition?

How wide is the printer?
What's the width of the printer?

How deep is the filing cabinet?
What's the depth of the filing cabinet?

How high is the desk?
What's the height of the desk?

Notice the following questions about dimensions in general:
How big is the desk?
What size is the desk?

3. Controlled practice

(a) What questions would you ask to get the following information? The first one has been done for you.

---

1. The length of the room
   How long is the room?
2. The general dimensions of the office
   What _____ _____ _____ _____?
3. The height of the window
   How _____ _____ _____ _____?
4. The depth of the drawer
   What _____ _____ _____ _____ _____ _____?
5. The general dimensions of the desk
   How _____ _____ _____ _____?
6. The width of the window
   How _____ _____ _____ _____?

(b) Now complete the following dialogue about the filing cabinet below:

140 cm

60 cm   80 cm

A: And we also sell a bigger filing cabinet.
B: Yes, I see. And how many drawers does it have?
A: This model has _____ _____.
B: How high is it?
A: Well, the _____ is _____ cm.
B: And what about the depth?
A: It's _____ cm _____.
B: And how wide is it?
A: Let me see. Yes, it's _____ cm _____ _____.
B: 60 cm. Well, in that case it's too _____ to fit in here.

4. Transfer

■ PAIR WORK
Student B: turn to the Key section.

Student A: you have been asked by your boss to find out details of the following items of furniture for his office:
(a) A desk to fit into location 'A'.
(b) A bookcase (to hold 200 catalogues) to fit into location 'B'.
(c) A filing cabinet to fit into location 'C'.

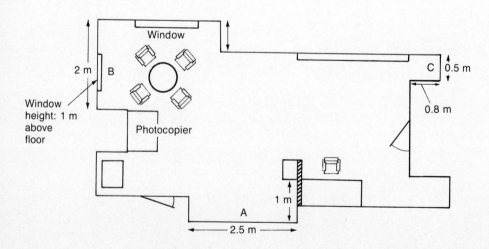

Student B is an office equipment supplier. Without showing the illustration of your boss's office:

tell the supplier what you are interested in;
ask what models of furniture are available;
find out their dimension and size;
answer questions about your boss's office;
discuss which items of furniture are most suitable.

5. Word check

equipment – desks, computers, filing cabinets, etc.
calculation – results reached by using numbers
filing cabinet – piece of office furniture for storing papers
specification – details of measurement
identical – exactly the same
shelf – board fixed to a wall for placing things on
to wobble – to move
keyboard – device, like a typewriter, to input information into a computer or word processor
to replace – to put a new thing in place of an old one
catalogue – book of products available
partition – movable wall in an office
privacy – state of being away from the presence of others
to hide – to keep out of sight

The International Trade Fair

(conditionals 1 and 2)

Introduction

Some time ago Compact Systems received details of the 'Info Trade Fair' to be held in Munich from 15th to 19th September. Hilary returned the form to book a stand, but hasn't heard anything.

1. Listening 🔘🔘

Alice Everett has asked Hilary Beacham to contact the fair organisers to check that all the arrangements for Compact's stand have been made. As you listen to the tape, indicate whether the following statements are true or false.

	True	False
1. Interfair rings Compact		
2. Hilary Beacham asks to speak to Frau Müller		
3. The trade fair is in September		
4. Herr Bernstein isn't available		
5. Hilary returned her registration form		
6. Hilary sent payment for a stand		
7. Bookings for stands are closed		
8. Herr Bernstein has one free stand		
9. Hilary wants a stand in the lobby		
10. Herr Bernstein asks Hilary to phone before 5 p.m.		

🔘🔘

2. Presentation

Here is some of the language you have just heard. The speakers use two types of conditional sentences.

(a) Condition	Result
If you hold on a minute,	I'll see if Herr Bernstein is available.
If your registration is correct,	I will have the details here.
If you give me the name of your company,	I will check for you.
If you hang on a minute,	I'll find out for you.
If you want to speak to Frau Müller	you must phone this number.
present tense	future with 'will' or modal, e.g. can, must, should, etc.

94

(b)	Condition	Result
	If you filled in your registration form correctly If I found a free stand, If there was one in the main concourse If you made your decision now,	I would have your name here. you would have to let me know today. we would prefer that. I could check the availability situation.
	past tense	conditional with 'would' or modal, e.g. 'could'.

The difference between (a) and (b) is based on the speaker's attitude. Both (a) and (b) express a relationship between a condition and a result. In (a), the speakers see the condition as a real possibility. In (b), the condition is seen as possible but more hypothetical or doubtful. (a) is a real condition (R); (b) is a hypothetical condition (H).

3. Controlled practice

Now look at the sentence parts below. On the left you have the condition, on the right the result and, in brackets, a letter (R or H). If there is an R (real), make a sentence based on model (a) above. If there is an H (hypothetical), make a sentence based on model (b).

	condition	*result*
1. (R)	You hang on	I check for you
2. (H)	He is available	He talks to you
3. (R)	You ring at 16.00	He is in the office
4. (R)	You don't call us	We call you
5. (H)	He speaks to you	He doesn't want to repeat everything
6. (H)	He doesn't check	He can't give you an answer
7. (R)	We send it today	It arrives tomorrow
8. (H)	You don't send it	It can't arrive
9. (H)	We have it	We let you know
10. (R)	The answer is yes	You can start tomorrow

4. Transfer

■   GROUP WORK

Discuss in your groups what will (real possibility) or would (hypothetical possibility) happen if:

    your boss leaves
    you are not promoted soon
    you won a lot of money
    your company went bankrupt

5. Word check

to hold on − to wait
to deal with − to take action on
enquiry − question
registration form − document to be filled in to make a booking
to enclose − to send a document in the same envelope as another document (e.g. to enclose a cheque with a letter)
to fill in (a form) − to complete
payment − money to pay for something
conditions − requirements, what you must do
invoice − bill
confirmed − firmly booked
stand − place for displaying things at a fair
(entrance) lobby − in a large building, the first area you walk into
main concourse − largest part of a big building
transfer − sending of money from one bank to another

Two important phone calls

(prediction and certainty)

Introduction

Alice Everett is away on a business trip. In the first call she rings Hilary Beacham in Compact's head office to find out what arrangements have been made for her trip to Glasgow. And in the second call Hilary phones the travel agent to check the availability of seats on planes to Glasgow.

1. Listening 🔲

Listen to the tape on which Alice Everett is speaking to Hilary Beacham about the trip to Glasgow. As you listen, show on the table below whether the statements below are true or false.

	True	False
The Hotel Regent can definitely fit Alice in from the 18th to the 22nd.		
The conference centre will certainly be available from 2.00 to 9.30 on the 18th.		
The Glasgow managers are likely to make the meeting on the 20th.		
The Edinburgh representatives certainly can't meet Alice on the 19th.		
The restaurant is likely to be available on the 19th.		

In the second call Hilary phones the travel agent to find out the times of planes to Glasgow and the availability of seats. As you listen complete the table. The first one has been done for you.

	Seat available?				
	Definitely	Probably	Possibly	Probably not	Definitely not
Flight times — 17th Dep. 17.00 Arr. 18.00 Dep. _____ Arr. _____					✔
Flight times — 18th Dep. _____ Arr. _____ Dep. _____ Arr. _____ Dep. _____ Arr. _____					

🔲

2. Presentation

	Scale of likelihood
Definitely (+ +)	sure I'm certain } you'll get a seat on that one. positive I'm certain } to get one on the 8 o'clock. bound The 17.00 is certainly } full definitely
Probably (+)	It's likely that the 18.00 will be full The 18.00 is likely to be full
Possibly (?)	may } get a seat on the 7 o'clock I might
Probably not (−)	It's unlikely that they will manage the 21st They're unlikely to manage the 21st
Certainly not (− −)	There definitely } won't be a seat available on that flight certainly sure You are certain } that I won't get a seat positive

3. Controlled practice

Alice is planning to stay on in Glasgow for two days to meet some of the sales reps. Below are Hilary's notes on their availability. Use appropriate expressions from above to complete the sentences. The first one has been done for you.

	Monday		Tuesday	
	a.m.	p.m.	a.m.	p.m.
In the office	Brian (+ +)	Brian (?)		—
In Glasgow	Chris (−) Enc. (+)	Eric (++)		
Available	Allan (− −)	Allan (− −) Derek (?)	Allan (−) Chris (−)	Derek (++)

1. Allan is unlikely to be available on Tuesday morning.
2. Brian _____ be in the office on Monday afternoon.
3. Chris _____ _____ to be in Glasgow on Monday morning.
4. Derek is _____ to be _____ on Tuesday afternoon.
5. It _____ _____ _____ Eric will be _____ _____ on Monday morning.
6. Allan _____ _____ _____ available on Monday.
7. Brian _____ _____ be _____ _____ _____ on Monday morning.
8. It _____ _____ that Chris _____ _____ _____ on Tuesday morning.
9. Derek _____ _____ _____ on Monday afternoon.
10. Eric _____ _____ _____ _____ _____ _____ on Monday afternoon.

4. Transfer

■ PAIR WORK

Before starting this activity, you may wish to refer to the telephone language in Appendix 1, p. 166.

Student B: turn to the Key section.

Student A: as Personal Assistant to Mr/s Hampton you have to arrange a meeting between him/her and Mr/s Bryce (the manager of another company) for the week beginning Monday 21st August. Your boss has said that the meeting will last a morning or an afternoon. Phone Mr/s Bryce and find out the best possible time for the meeting. Here is the relevant page from your boss's diary:

	a.m.	p.m.
Monday 21st	Meeting with sales reps (+ +)	
Tuesday 22nd	Trade fair in London (+)	Trade fair (+)
Wednesday 23rd	Meeting with Financial Director (+)	
Thursday 24th		Demonstration by Sofpac (?)
Friday 25th	Department meeting (+ +)	Leave about 3 p.m. (+)

5. Word check

hectic — very busy
party — group of people
packed out — completely full
conference centre — building for conferences
to book — to reserve a hotel room, flight, etc.
availability — free seats on a plane
up-to-date — current, most recent
seat — place on a plane, train, etc.

End-of-year report

(quantity and amount)

Introduction

In Compact March is the last month of the trading year. As this month approaches, it is time to prepare the end-of-year report, which gives an overview of the company's performance. In Compact each department prepares its own report on its activities.

1a. Reading

Alice Everett has prepared a draft of the end-of-year report from the Marketing Department, and has asked Karen Williams to type it up. Read through the extract below, and as you read put a tick (✔) in the True column if the information in the table is correct, or in the False column if the information is incorrect.

	True	*False*
The main cause of personnel changes is low pay.		
Many secretaries have left for better-paid jobs.		
Alice Everett does not want to hold a pay review.		
There have been several negative responses to the questionnaire.		
Much useful information was gained from the questionnaire.		
None of the replies were interested in the product.		
The conference went very well.		
Most of the discussion was about China.		
Some of the company's products have been unsuccessful.		

END-OF-YEAR REPORT FOR THE PERIOD 1 APRIL 19—— TO 30 MARCH 19——

1. Personnel in the Marketing Department
We have seen many personnel changes in the Marketing Department during the past year. Most of the changes have been caused by retirement, but some of our key employees have moved to better-paid jobs.
  Also, in the typing pool many of our secretaries have been tempted to move to other companies and better salaries. I recommend that we hold a review of general pay and conditions in the Marketing Department to try to prevent this problem re-occurring.

2. Market research
The results of our questionnaire have now been collected and a detailed analysis can be found in Appendix 1. In brief, none of the responses were negative and a lot of them gave very useful information. The exercise was therefore well worthwhile. A few of the replies even expressed a definite interest in ordering large numbers of our products.

3. Annual conference
This year's conference was held in Bath, and all the delegates thought it was a great success. Much of the discussion focused on trade with European countries and a little concerned trade with China.

4. Sales performance
All of the company's products have had a successful year. Perhaps more important . . .

1b. Listening 🔘

Alice has now looked through the above report, and has decided to make a few changes. As you listen to the conversation between Alice and Hilary Beacham, make the necessary changes to the above extract from the end-of-year report.

2. Presentation

Here is some of the language you have just read. Notice how it is used to express quantity and amount.

	0	20%	50%	75%	90%	100%
any noun	none of		some of	a lot of	most of	all (of)
count nouns		a few of		many of		
mass nouns		a little of		much of		

Now look at the following example sentences.
All the delegates considered it a great success.
Most of the changes have been caused by retirement.
A lot gave very useful information.
Many of our secretaries have been tempted to move.
Much of the discussion focused on trade with European countries.
Some of our key employees have moved to better-paid jobs.
A few of the replies expressed definite interest.
A little of it concerned trade with China.
None of the responses were negative.

3. Controlled practice

Now look at the following letter which is sent out to Compact's investors with the annual report. Complete the letter using an appropriate quantity/amount word or phrase.

COMPACT SYSTEMS
96 Rosewall Drive, Southtown, SO3 4BT

Dear Investor,

I am sure that _ _ _ _ _ _ you will already have read in the papers that this year has been another good year for Compact. Without exception, _ _ _ _ _ _ our products have performed well in Europe – _ _ _ _ _ _ them, of course, better than others. From modest beginnings with only _ _ _ _ _ _ salesmen, we now have an extensive sales force both in the UK and abroad. As a result we now cover _ _ _ _ _ _ European countries, and hope to extend our activities to the Far East in the near future. In order to make our whole selling team more effective we intend to give _ _ _ _ _ _ them an opportunity to improve their sales techniques. _ _ _ _ _ _ will follow training courses in Southtown, and others will be sent to centres in London. So, as you can see, _ _ _ _ _ _ money will be invested in training in the future.

We had _ _ _ _ _ _ small problems at our Southtown factory early in the year due to delayed deliveries from the Far East which _ _ _ _ _ _ us could have foreseen. However, I am glad to inform you that they have now been resolved.

We look forward to another successful year.

David Burton.

David Burton
Managing Director

4. Transfer

■ GROUP WORK

Look at the following duties of Personal Assistant and secretaries. Discuss how much of your time is devoted to these activities, and how much of other colleagues in your company.

Answering the phone
Drafting letters
Typing letters
Taking dictation
Receiving visitors
Attending meetings
Writing the minutes of meetings
Handling the mail
Instructing others
Other activities

Here are some examples:

I answer a lot of telephone calls.
I only answer a few telephone calls, but I draft a lot of letters.
I also draft a lot of letters and also answer some of the telephone calls.

5. Word check

trading year – financial year
draft – first plan of a document
personnel – people employed in a company
retirement – act of stopping work because one has reached a certain age
key – most important
typing pool – group of typists working together in a company
to tempt – to attract
salary – pay
to prevent – to stop
to re-occur – to happen again
market research – gathering of statistics before a new product is designed
questionnaire – printed list of questions, especially used in market research
analysis – detailed examination and report
response – reply
worthwhile – useful
delegate – person who represents others at a meeting
to edit – to change a document

KEY SECTION   Units 1—26

This section contains:

i   tapescripts and keys to the Listening and/or Reading exercises
ii   answers to the Controlled practice exercises
iii   information for the Transfer section where required

Job advertisements and applications

1a. Reading

	COMPACT SYSTEMS			INVENTOR PLUS		
	NECESSARY	NOT NECESSARY	PROHIBITED	NECESSARY	NOT NECESSARY	PROHIBITED
have experience of working in a computer company	✔			✔		
have typing and shorthand skills		✔		✔		
have a minimum of five years' work experience	✔			✔		
have two referees	✔				✔	
be willing to travel		✔		✔		
send a full c.v.	✔			✔		
be under 28			✔	✔		

1b. Listening 🔊

Tapescript

HB: Hey! Look at this. Here's an advertisement for a Personal Assistant.

ED: Here's another one — Inventor Plus. Have you heard of them?

HB: No, but I have heard of Compact Systems. They're supposed to be very good to work for, and computer companies are my line exactly.

ED: Are you going to apply for it?

HB: I will, I think. Look at this. It says, 'Must provide two referees and a statement of what makes a good PA or secretary.'

ED: What do you think they mean?

HB: I don't know. Perhaps they mean things like filing systems.

ED: Oh yes, a good PA has to have a good filing system.

HB: Can you think of anything else?

ED: Well, you could say something about receiving visitors. 'An effective Personal Assistant must be good at receiving visitors,' something like that.

HB: I agree, you mustn't create a bad impression.

ED: Well, that's two things. What else?

HB: I know! A good PA must also distribute work fairly to other typists.

ED: And what about phone manner?

HB: Yes, of course. You've got to have a good phone manner.

ED: And there's appearance. In the last place I worked we had to dress very neatly.

HB: OK, that's the fifth one: a good PA must also have a neat appearance. Can you think of any more?

ED: No, I think those are the most important points.

Answers to the listening task

1. Have a good filing system.
2. Be good at receiving visitors.
3. Distribute work fairly to other typists.
4. Have a good phone manner.
5. Have a neat appearance.

<hr>

[▭▭]

3. Controlled practice

2. Candidates don't need/have to be prepared to travel overseas.
3. Candidates have (got) to know how to use a computer.
4. Candidates mustn't be over 30.
5. Candidates have got to speak German.
6. Candidates don't need to be able to work at weekends.
7. Candidates have (got) to be prepared to travel overseas.
8. Candidates must know how to use a computer.
9. Candidates have (got) to be over 30.
10. Candidates needn't/don't need to/don't have to/haven't got to speak German.

4. Transfer

Model letter

COMPACT SYSTEMS
96 Rosewall Drive, Southtown, SO3 4BT

63 Wenwell Gardens
Southtown
SO9 7PX

12 January 19———

Dear Sir/Madam

I am writing in response to your advertisement for a Personal Assistant/Secretary to assist departmental managers in your Southtown office.

I am enclosing a copy of my curriculum vitae, which gives details of my qualifications and experience. As you will see I have had 12 years' job experience, including two in a computer company. I also have an RSA Stage III in Typing and RSA 100 w.p.m. Shorthand.

In my opinion a good PA/Secretary must:

    have a good filing system;
    be good at receiving visitors;
    distribute work fairly to other typists;
    have a good phone manner;
    have a neat appearance.

I will be available for interview at any time, and look forward to hearing from you.

Yours faithfully

Hilary Beacham

Hilary Beacham

The interview

1. Listening ⟨🔊⟩

Tapescript

PM: Personnel Manager
MM: Marketing Manager
HB: Hilary Beacham

PM: Come in. Ah, good morning Miss Beacham. Thank you for coming.
HB: Good morning.
PM: Please sit down.
HB: Thank you.
PM: Can I introduce you to Alice Everett, our Marketing Manager.
HB: How do you do?
MM: How do you do?
PM: And I am Sheila Polson, the Personnel Manager. So, Miss Beacham, did you find us easily this morning?
HB: Yes, it's an easy route from where I live in Southtown.
PM: And do you have your own car?
HB: Yes, I have.
PM: Good. Can we check on a few of your personal details? You were born in 1953, is that right?
HB: Yes, 3rd September 1953 to be exact.
PM: And you're single.
HB: Yes, I am.
PM: OK. Can we move on to your education now? You've got four 'O' levels including English language?
HB: That's right.
PM: Thank you very much, Miss Beacham. Alice, would you like to continue?
MM: Yes, certainly. Miss Beacham, can you tell us a little bit about where you have worked before?
HB: Well, my last job was with Format.
MM: And you were a PA there?
HB: Yes, that's right.
MM: And when did you start with them?
HB: Two years ago.
MM: I see. So why did you decide to leave?
HB: Well, perhaps you heard that the company went into liquidation earlier this year.
MM: Yes, we heard about it.
PM: So what did you like about that job?
HB: Well, my job was PA to the Marketing Manager. What I enjoyed most was coming into contact with customers and suppliers both face-to-face and on the phone.
MM: And where did you work before Format?
HB: Ideal Systems.
MM: And how long did you work for Ideal Systems?
HB: For ten years, as a secretary.
PM: And why did you leave that job?
HB: Well, I felt that I needed a change. I think I had learnt all I could there.

MM: Going back to Format. Who did you work for there?
HB: A man called Peter Smith. Do you know him?
MM: We've met. OK, that's enough on work experience. Do you have any word-processing experience?
HB: Yes, as a secretary at Ideal Systems I used a word-processing system designed by the company. It was called 'Word'.
MM: And what about at Format? That was also a computer company, wasn't it?
HB: Yes, that's right.
MM: So how much experience do you have of working in computer companies?
HB: Well, two years at Format and ten at Ideal Systems. Oh, and I also had some work experience with a software company while I was at college.
PM: What secretarial qualifications did you get while you were at college?
HB: Well I've got two secretarial qualifications. I've got RSA Stage III Typing.
PM: So your typing should be pretty good?
HB: Well, in fact I didn't do much typing at Format. I've got an RSA in shorthand.
PM: And which qualification exactly?
HB: The RSA 100 ... so 100 words per minute.
PM: Fine. And one final question. If we decided to offer you the job, when could you start?
HB: Oh, I could start immediately, or as soon as you wanted me to.
PM: Fine. I think that's everything. Have you got any questions?
HB: Well, I would like to know ...

Answers to the listening task

```
                          CURRICULUM VITAE

PERSONAL
Name:            Hilary Beacham
Address:         63 Wenwell Gardens
                 Southtown
Date of birth:   3rd September 1953
Marital status:  Single

EDUCATION
GCE 'O' LEVELS:    English Language
                   Mathematics
                   Biology
                   Geography

RSA:               RSA Stage III Typing
                   RSA 100 w.p.m. Shorthand

PROFESSIONAL EXPERIENCE

Company          Position        Length of service    Reason for leaving

1. Ideal Systems  Secretary       10 years            Needed a change
2. Format         PA to MM        2 years             Liquidation of
                                                      company
```

3. Controlled practice

2. When did you get your secretarial qualifications?
3. Why did you leave your last job?
4. How did you travel to work?
5. Who did you work for?
6. How long did you live there?
7. How long did the meeting last?
8. What did you study?
9. How many letters did you usually type a day?
10. Where did you work?

4. Transfer

(a) **Student B:** ask your partner questions in order to complete the brief c.v. below.

```
┌─────────────────────────────────────────────────────────────────────────┐
│                          CURRICULUM VITAE                                 │
│                                                                           │
│   PERSONAL                                                                │
│   Name:              _ _ _ _ _ _ _ _ _ _ _ _ _ _                          │
│   Date of birth:     _ _ _ _ _ _ _ _ _ _ _ _ _ _                          │
│   Marital status:    _ _ _ _ _ _ _ _ _ _ _ _ _ _                          │
│                                                                           │
│   EDUCATION                                                               │
│   Dates              Institutions                                         │
│   _____ - _____    _ _ _ _ _ _ _ _ _ _ _ _ _ _                          │
│   _____ - _____    _ _ _ _ _ _ _ _ _ _ _ _ _ _                          │
│                                                                           │
│   Secretarial qualifications                                              │
│   Dates              Qualifications                                       │
│   _____             _ _ _ _ _ _ _ _ _ _ _ _ _ _                          │
│   _____             _ _ _ _ _ _ _ _ _ _ _ _ _ _                          │
│   _____             _ _ _ _ _ _ _ _ _ _ _ _ _ _                          │
│   _____             _ _ _ _ _ _ _ _ _ _ _ _ _ _                          │
│   _____             _ _ _ _ _ _ _ _ _ _ _ _ _ _                          │
│                                                                           │
│   PROFESSIONAL EXPERIENCE                                                  │
│   Company        Position        Length of service     Reason for leaving │
│                                                                           │
│   1. _ _ _ _ _   _ _ _ _ _ _ _ _ _ _ _ _ _ _ _ _ _ _   _ _ _ _ _ _        │
│   2. _ _ _ _ _   _ _ _ _ _ _ _ _ _ _ _ _ _ _ _ _ _ _   _ _ _ _ _ _        │
└─────────────────────────────────────────────────────────────────────────┘
```

(b) **Student B:** your partner is going to ask you questions about your education, qualifications and job experience. Answer the questions so that your partner can complete your c.v.

UNIT 3 Day 1: Meeting office staff

1. Listening 🔘

Tapescript

HB: Hilary Beacham
PM: Personnel Manager
OM: Office Manager
MM: Marketing Manager
PA: Personal Assistant
Sec: Secretary
FC: Filing Clerk

PM: Ah, good morning, Hilary. And how are you?

HB: Very well, thank you. And you?

PM: Yes, I'm fine. First of all I think we should go round and meet some of the staff you'll be working with. Let's start with your boss, Alice Everett. I'm sure you'll remember her from the interview. Now, you'll be working with her for the first two months.

HB: Yes, I see.

MM: Come in.

PM: Good morning, Alice. I'm just showing Hilary round . . . doing the introductions, before she starts working with you.

MM: Good morning, Hilary. Nice to see you again.

PM: Now, you'll start working with Alice from next week. In the second part of this week George will be showing you how everything's done, so that you know your way around.

MM: Fine. So, I'll look forward to seeing you next week, Hilary.

HB: Yes, I'm looking forward to working with you, Mrs Everett.

PM: Good. Let's move on to the General Office.

PM: Good morning, everyone. Can I have a few moments of your time? I'd like to introduce a new member of staff. First things first, I'd like to introduce you to our Office Manager. You'll be spending today and tomorrow with her.

OM: Pleased to meet you, my name's Christine Adams.

HB: How do you do? I'm Hilary Beacham.

PM: Hilary. Let me introduce you two. Mr Brown, this is Hilary.

HB: How do you do? My name's Beacham. Hilary Beacham.

PA: George Brown.

PM: George is Mrs Everett's Personal Assistant. He'll be showing you how everything works before he leaves us at the end of the week and you take his place. Let's move on, shall we? Hilary, this is Helen Wright.

Sec.: Hello, Hilary. How are you doing?

HB: Fine, thanks, Helen.

PM: You know each other, do you?

HB: Yes, very well. Helen is one of my best friends.

PM: Anyway, as you probably know, Helen is one of the secretaries. And Miss Hobday . . .

FC: Hello, my name's Sally.

HB: Nice to meet you. Mine's Hilary.

FC: I'm the filing clerk.

PM: Hilary, this is Karen Williams. Alice Everett has two secretaries working for her, and Karen is one of them.

FC: Nice to meet you.

PM: I think that's enough for the moment. Now then, let's have a look at the office equipment. Christine, could you tell Hilary a bit about the equipment we use?

Answers to the listening task

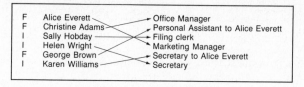

111

3. Controlled practice

1. 'Good evening, Mr Simmons. How are you?'
   'Very well, thank you. And you?'
2. 'I'd like to introduce you to Mr Hampshire.'
   'Pleased to meet you. My name's Askwith, Susan Askwith.'
3. 'Paul, this is Erica.'
   'Nice to meet you.'
4. 'Hello, Peter. How are you?'
   'I'm fine. And you?'
5. 'Hello, my name's Paula.'
   'Nice to meet you. Mine's Gordon.'
6. 'How do you do? I'm Harriet Arnold.'
   'How do you do? My name's Brown, Michael Brown.'
7. 'Let me introduce you two. Mr Bryce, this is Mr Derry.'

UNIT 4 Day 1: Getting to know the equipment

1. Reading

Answers to the reading task

Equipment	Function	Advantage(s)
1. Word processor	displays text on a screen	(i) you can see the whole text (ii) easy and quick to correct mistakes
2. Dictating machine	it is used for recording letters onto tape	(i) secretaries don't need to take dictation
3. Telex	it is used for sending and receiving messages	(i) available day and night (ii) inexpensive
4. Facsimile machine	it is for sending copies of documents, pictures, etc.	(i) quicker than posting

3. Controlled practice

Equipment	Function
(1) stapler	(7) stick one piece of paper to another.
(2) hole punch	(1) fix pieces of paper together.
(3) ruler	(6) make holes in paper stronger.
(4) Tippex fluid	(8) erase mistakes.
(5) paper clips	(2) make holes in paper.
(6) reinforcement rings	(4) correct mistakes.
(7) paper glue	(3) draw straight lines.
(8) rubber	(9) sharpen pencils.
(9) pencil sharpener	(5) hold pieces of paper together.

1. This is a stapler. It is used for fixing pieces of paper together.
2. This is a hole punch. It makes holes in paper.
3. This is a ruler. It is used for drawing straight lines.
4. This is Tippex fluid. It is for correcting mistakes.

5. These are paper clips. They hold pieces of paper together.
6. These are reinforcement rings. They are used for making holes in paper stronger.
7. This is paper glue. It is for sticking one piece of paper to another.
8. This is a rubber. It is (used) for erasing mistakes.
9. This is a pencil sharpener. It is used for sharpening pencils.

UNIT 5 Who's who in the company

1. Listening 🔘🔘

Tapescript

AE: I think I'd better take this opportunity to explain to you exactly who's who in the company. You'll need to know who to go to if you want to contact a particular manager. Let's start right at the top: David Burton is the Managing Director and his Personal Assistant is Mary Wilkins. The company is divided into four departments: Production, Personnel, Marketing and Finance. OK?

HB: Uh-huh.

AE: Right. Let's deal with each one in turn. Michael Stott looks after Production, and his title is Production Manager, and Daniel Harkin works as Personal Assistant in the Production Department. Then there are two secretaries. Is that clear?

HB: Yes.

AE: Moving on to Personnel, we've got Sheila Polson, and her title is Personnel Director. Jane Hargreaves works for Sheila Polson as Personal Assistant. And then there are two secretaries in the department. OK?

HB: Yes, fine.

AE: As you know, I'm the Marketing Manager and for the next two months you are going to work as my Personal Assistant. Helen Wright and Karen Williams, the two secretaries in the department, will report to you. Is that clear?

HB: Uh-huh.

AE: And finally . . . Paul Cummins is responsible for the Finance Department. His PA is Judith Walker. And then there are three secretaries in the department. You've met one already, I think. So that's a brief overview of the structure of the company. Do you have any questions? . . .

Answers to the listening task

Compact Systems — company structure

	Name: David Burton Title: Managing Director PA: Mary Wilkins		
Name: Michael Stott	Name: Sheila Polson	Name: Alice Everett	Name: Paul Cummins
Title: Production Manager	Title: Personnel Director	Title: Marketing Manager	Title: Financial Director
PA: Daniel Harkin	PA: Jane Hargreaves	PA: Hilary Beacham	PA: Judith Walker
2 secretaries	2 secretaries	2 secretaries	3 secretaries

3. Controlled practice

2. Paul Cummins is the Financial Director.
3. Jane Hargreaves works for the Personnel Director.
4. Two secretaries work under Daniel Harkin in the Production Department.
5. Alice Everett reports to the Managing Director.
6. Michael Stott is responsible for the Production Department.
7. Hilary Beacham works in the Marketing Department.
8. Paul Cummins looks after the Finance Department.

4. Transfer

(a) **Student B:** your partner is going to describe the structure of Whitney Industrials. Complete the diagram below. Then compare diagrams.

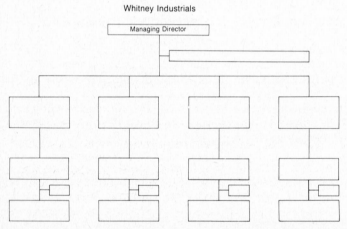

Whitney Industrials

(b) **Student B:** Below is the company structure of Wolverhampton Agrochem. Describe it to your partner who will fill in his/her diagram. After you have finished compare your diagrams.

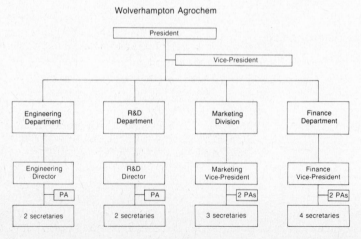

Wolverhampton Agrochem

Checking arrangements

---

1. Listening 🔘────────────────────────────

Tapescript

Call 1
- S: CTM, güten Tag.
- HB: Good morning. Can I speak to Mr Günther Harz, please?
- S: Who's calling, please?
- HB: My name is Hilary Beacham from Compact Systems.
- S: One moment, please. I will connect you.
- GH: Harz.
- HB: Good morning, Mr Harz. This is Hilary Beacham from Compact Systems here.
- GH: Ah, good morning, Mrs Beacham.
- HB: Mr Harz, I'm ringing to check your travel details for your visit to Compact next week. I need to find out when you intend to arrive so we can make the necessary arrangements for your stay. Now, the meeting will be on the 28th February.
- GH: To be honest, I have a bit of a problem about the meeting. Something important has come up here and I might not be able to come, if I can't solve it this week. But let's hope I can. So I'll give you the details now. Now . . . I'm planning to arrive on the 27th.
- HB: I see.
- GH: The flight number is LF 129 and it arrives at 14.30.
- HB: That's a Lufthansa flight, isn't it?
- GH: Yes, and I am coming into Gatwick.
- HB: I think that's all I need to know. Thank you. Goodbye.
- GH: Goodbye.

Call 2
- S: Studio Centro.
- HB: Ricardo Garniga, please.
- S: One moment, please.
- RG: Garniga.
- HB: Good morning, Mr Garniga. Hilary Beacham from Compact Systems here.
- RG: Ah, from Compact Systems?
- HB: That's right. I'm calling to find out your travel arrangements for the meeting on the 28th.
- RG: Ah yes, the meeting at Compact. One moment, please. I'll just check with my assistant. (*pause*) Hello.
- HB: Hello.
- RG: She says that we are arriving on the 26th.
- HB: I'm sorry, did you say we?
- RG: Yes. I'm sure I told you that my assistant might come with me.
- HB: I'm afraid I didn't know anything about it. This is rather short notice. I may have problems finding accommodation for her.
- RG: Anyway, I'll talk it over and let you know this afternoon if she is definitely coming.
- HB: Fine. Could you tell me when your flight arrives?
- RG: At 10.00 on the morning of the 26th.

HB: The 26th?

RG: Yes. Is that too early? Should I arrive on the 27th?

HB: No, you needn't change your plans. I will make the necessary hotel arrangements for you. By the way, is that Gatwick airport?

RG: No, Heathrow. And the flight number is BA 322. A British Airways flight.

HB: Fine. Well, that's all for now. Thank you very much. Goodbye.

RG: Goodbye.

Call 3

S: Intersoft. Good morning.

HB: This is Hilary Beacham from Compact Systems in the UK. Could I speak to Martin Feldman, please?

S: Just one moment, please.

MF: Martin Feldman.

HB: Ah, hello Mr Feldman. Hilary Beacham from Compact Systems.

MF: Good. I wanted to talk to you about this meeting. I arrive at Heathrow at 6.15 p.m. on the 27th.

HB: Fine.

MF: I might be able to catch an earlier flight.

HB: Perhaps if you can inform us of any changes.

MF: Do I need to make a hotel reservation?

HB: No, I will make all the arrangements.

MF: Am I staying at the Imperial again?

HB: I'm afraid they may not have any rooms available this time.

MF: Oh dear! I must have a room with a telephone.

HB: I can't see a problem there, Mr Feldman. I'm sure we can find you a very comfortable hotel.

MF: And will I be met at the airport?

HB: Yes, our driver will meet your flight.

MF: Well, please tell your driver not to be late. I don't like to be kept waiting.

HB: Do you know the flight number?

MF: Yes, I have it here. It's a TWA flight, number TW 360.

HB: And that's on the 27th.

MF: That's right.

HB: Well, that's all, Mr Feldman. Thank you very much.

MF: Goodbye.

HB: Goodbye.

Answers to the listening task

	Phone call		
	1	2	3
Name:	Günther Harz	Ricardo Garniga	Martin Feldman
Arrival date:	27th February	26th February	27th February
Airport:	Gatwick	Heathrow	Heathrow
Airline:	Lufthansa	British Airways	TWA
Flight number:	LF 129	BA 322	TW 360
Time:	2.30 p.m.	10.00 a.m.	6.15 p.m.

3. Controlled practice

AP: Fine thanks, and you? (9)
S: Who's calling, please? (3)
AP: Well, thanks very much for the information. (12)
AP: Could I speak to Sally Jones, please? (2)
AP: Hello, Sally. This is Ann Pilkington here. (7)
SJ: Not at all. (13)
SJ: Oh, hello Ann. How are you? (8)
S: MIB. Good morning. (1)
AP: Sally, I'm ringing to ask if you can recommend a good ... (11)
AP: My name is Ann Pilkington. (4)
AP: 'Bye. (14/15)
SJ: Yes, fine, too. (10)
S: One moment, please. (5)
SJ: 'Bye. (14/15)
SJ: Sally Jones. (6)

4. Transfer

(a) **Student B:** you work in the Scottish office of ABT. In this activity you will need to play two roles:
    the switchboard of ABT
    the PA/secretary who has just collected the air tickets below.
In the activity you need to carry out the following steps:
    answer the phone and identify your company (from the switchboard)
    find out the caller's identity (from the switchboard)
    connect the caller (from the switchboard)
    identify yourself (as PA/secretary)
    give the relevant information (as PA/secretary)
    end the call (as PA/secretary)

Itinerary prepared for: *Mr. John Walker*

Flight information: all times indicated are local

Date	Flight number	Airport check in	Time	Departure time	Arrival time
27 Feb.	BM 407	Edinburgh	16.00	16.30	17.30
1 March	BM 502	London HR	19.30	20.00	21.00

Itinerary prepared for: *Mr. Paul Roberts*					
Flight information: all times indicated are local					

Date	Flight number	Airport check in	Time	Departure time	Arrival time
27 Feb	BM 402	Edinburgh	17.30	18.00	19.00
2 March	BM 523	London HR	07.30	08.00	09.00

(b) **Student B:** your boss has given you the following list of key participants for your company's annual international sales conference, and has asked you to check that the starred names are coming. Ring the company and complete your table below.

Remember to:

request your correspondent
identify yourself
explain the purpose of your call
thank your correspondent for the information
end the call

Name	Company	Arrival date	Flight number	Time	Departure date	Flight number	Time
Harz, Günther	CTM	27 Feb.	LF 129	14.30	1 March	BA 306	17.30
Garniga, Ricardo	SC	26 Feb.	BA 322	10.00	1 March	IB 438	18.00
Feldman, Martin	IS	27 Feb.	TW 360	18.15	?	?	?
Lloyd, George*	ABT						
Tober, Eric*	ABT						

UNIT 7 Booking a hotel room

1a. Reading

Answers to the reading task

	Requirements
1.	Room available on 5th, 6th and 7th May
2.	Telephone
3.	Near Lancaster Road
4.	Meeting room
5.	Restaurant

1b. Listening 🔘🔘

Tapescript

Hotel 1

L: Lancaster Hotel.

HB: Hello. My name is Hilary Beacham from Compact Systems. I'd like some information, please.

L: Sorry. You'll have to speak up: it's a very bad line.

HB: OK. Can you tell me if you have any single rooms available on the 5th, 6th and 7th May?

L: Sorry. I didn't quite catch those dates.

HB: The 5th, 6th and 7th May.

L: Yes, we still have rooms for those dates.

HB: And does every room have a telephone?

L: Oh yes.

HB: And the location is very important. Are you near Lancaster Road?

L: Well, we're actually in Lancaster Road. Number 16.

HB: *(writing)* 60 Lancaster Road.

L: Excuse me. Not '60' − 16.

HB: 16 − thank you. And the next question is: do you have any meeting rooms?

L: Can you repeat that please?

HB: Meetings rooms. Do you have any?

L: We do. I'll just check that we have one available for those dates ... Yes, we do.

HB: Good.

L: Is there anything else?

HB: Oh yes. Is there a restaurant in the hotel?

L: Did you say 'restaurant'?

HB: That's right.

L: No, I'm afraid not; just a snack bar. But there are a number of excellent ones just round the corner.

HB: OK. Thanks very much. Goodbye.

L: Goodbye.

Hotel 2

G: Goodwood Hotel.

HB: Hello. I'd like some information, please.

G: Go ahead.

HB: Do your rooms all have telephones?

G: They do, yes.

HB: And is there a meeting room available?

G: We do have a meeting room. I'd have to check that it's available for the dates you need.

HB: The 5th, 6th and 7th May.
 G: Let me see. Yes, that's fine.
HB: And do you have a restaurant?
 G: No, I'm afraid not.
HB: Oh, I see. And where is the hotel?
 G: We're in Burton Road.
HB: Is that near Lancaster Road.
 G: Not really. We're actually about two miles from Lancaster Road. What days did you say you wanted to book?
HB: 5th, 6th and 7th, but ...
 G: The 5th ...
HB: ... 6th and 7th.
 G: I'm sorry. We're actually booked solid for those dates.
HB: OK. Thank you.
 G: Goodbye.
HB: 'Bye.

Hotel 3
 X: Hello.
HB: Good afternoon. Is that the Burberry?
 X: I'm afraid you've got the wrong number. This is 659 1033.
HB: Oh, sorry.

HB: 6-5-9 1-0-2-3
 B: The Burberry Hotel. Good afternoon.
HB: Good afternoon. Can you tell me if you have a single room for the nights of the 5th, 6th and 7th May?
 B: I'll just check for you. Yes, we can certainly fit you in for those dates.
HB: And where is the hotel exactly?
 B: In Tregarron Road.
HB: Can you spell that, please?
 B: Certainly. T-R-E-G-A-R-R-O-N.
HB: Thanks. Is that near Lancaster Road?
 B: Yes, it's just off Lancaster Road.
HB: And do the rooms have telephones?
 B: Yes.
HB: And do you have any meeting rooms?
 B: We do, yes.
HB: Is one available on those dates?
 B: I'll just check ... Yes, we have one free for all those dates.
HB: And are there any restaurant facilities?
 B: We do have our own restaurant facilities, yes.
HB: Thank you. That's all I need to know. Goodbye.
 B: Goodbye.

Answers to the listening task

Requirements	Hotel 1	Hotel 2	Hotel 3
1.	✓	X	✓
2.	✓	✓	✓
3.	✓	X	✓
4.	✓	✓	✓
5.	X	X	✓

3. Controlled practice

2. I'm afraid you've made a mistake. The flight leaves at 9.58.
3. Excuse me. Not fifty — fifteen.
4. I'm afraid you've made a mistake. Mr Little lives at 206 South Parade.
5. That's not quite right. His name is Dwite: D-W-I-T-E.
6. I'm afraid you've made a mistake. The total profits are £28,313.
7. Excuse me. Not second right — third right.

4. Transfer

Tapescript |oo| ————————————————————————————————

Boss: Take this letter, please Maria. It's to Mr D.P. Broadham ...
M: Can you spell that, please?
B: B-R-O-A-D-H-A-M — 106 Field Rise, Manchester. You can check the postcode yourself after. Just hang on a minute. That's not quite right. That should be 116 Field Rise. OK? 'Dear David'. No, change that to 'Dear Mr Broadham. Thank you for your letter of 13th May ...'
M: ... 30th May?
B: Excuse me. That's not quite right. It should be 13th May.
M: Sorry.
B: 'I'm sorry it has taken me so long to reply, but I have been overseas'. New paragraph. 'I confirm that 2,260 units will be available ...'
M: Can you repeat that, please?
B: Yes. '2,260 units will be available for delivery on 3rd July.'
M: Did you say the 3rd?
B: That's right. 'The total invoice will be for £21,400 ...'
M: Sorry. I didn't quite catch that.
B: 'The total invoice will be for £21,400 and we agree to accept payment after delivery.' Finish it 'Yours sincerely' and 'S.M. Cork, Sales Manager'.

———————————————————————————————————— |oo|

Answer to transfer task

Mr D.P. Broadham
116 Field Rise
Manchester

Dear Mr Broadham

Thank you for your letter of 13th May. I'm sorry it has taken me so long to reply, but I have been overseas.

I confirm that 2,260 units will be available for delivery on 3rd July. The total invoice will be for £21,400, and we agree to accept payment after delivery.

Yours sincerely

S.M. Cork
Sales Manager

Receiving visitors

1. Listening 🔘

Tapescript

JB: Good morning.

HB: Good morning.

JB: My name is John Brown. I have an appointment with Alice Everett at 11 o'clock.

HB: Yes, Mr Brown. Mrs Everett is expecting you. She'll be with you in a few minutes.

JB: Fine.

HB: Can I take your coat?

JB: Yes please. Here you are.

HB: Would you like to take a seat while you're waiting?

JB: No thanks. I've been sitting for the last three hours, and I'd like to stretch my legs.

HB: Can I get you something to drink — coffee, tea or a cold drink?

JB: Yes, that would be very nice. Could I have a cup of coffee, please?

HB: Yes, certainly, Mr Brown. How do you take it?

JB: White with one sugar.

HB: Fine. Sally, could you get Mr Brown a cup of coffee, please — white with one sugar.

S: Yes, certainly.

JB: While I'm waiting, perhaps we could sort a couple of things out.

HB: Uh-huh.

JB: This morning before I left the office I tried to make a reservation at this hotel ... the Grosvenor.

HB: Yes.

JB: ... but I couldn't get through. I think I'd better call them to make a reservation for tonight.

HB: Would you like me to call them for you?

JB: Yes, that's very kind of you.

HB: Shall I call a taxi to take you round there after your meeting with Mrs Everett?

JB: Is the hotel far?

HB: About fifteen minutes' walk from here.

JB: Thank you, but it's not necessary. I can easily walk.

S: Here's your coffee, Mr Brown.

JB: Thanks.

S: Would you like a biscuit?

JB: Thank you, but no.

HB: How long are you going to stay in Southtown, Mr Brown?

JB: I'll be here until tomorrow afternoon.

HB: Well, if there's anything else I can do for you, just ask me.

JB: That's very kind of you. Thank you.

HB: Yes ... yes. Mr Brown is here to see you. ... OK. Mr Brown, Mrs Everett is ready now. Please come this way.

JB: Right. Thank you.

Answers to the listening task

Offer	Accept	Decline
to take Mr Brown's coat	✔	
to sit down		✔
to have a drink	✔	
to call the hotel	✔	
to call a taxi		✔
to have a biscuit		✔

---

3. Controlled practice

(a)
2. Shall/can I take your coat?
3. Would you like me to reserve a table for you?
4. Would you like to take an earlier flight?
5. Can I do anything else for you?

(b)
1. Can I get you a drink?
   Yes please.
2. Would you like a biscuit?
   No thank you.
3. Would you like me to book a taxi?
   Thank you, but no.
4. Would you like to go to the theatre tonight?
   Yes, that would be very nice.
5. Would you like me to collect you from the hotel tomorrow?
   Thank you, but it's not necessary.

4. Transfer

■ PAIR WORK
(a) **Student B:** it is 11 o'clock. You are Mr/s Klein from Germany. You have an appointment with Mr Green.
   introduce yourself;
   explain that you have an appointment with Mr Green;
   accept or decline the offers;
   explain you need to reschedule your 12 o'clock appointment with Mr Grundy at
      Interco to 3 o'clock;
   explain that you've lost the details of the hotel where you should stay;

explain that you need to change some money;

explain that your luggage is still at the airport;

explain that you need to confirm your return flight for tomorrow evening at 17.00.

(b) **Student B:** it is 11 o'clock. Your boss is expecting Mr/s de Miguel from Spain. When Mr/s de Miguel arrives:

introduce yourself;

explain that your boss will be free in a few minutes;

offer to take his/her coat;

invite him/her to sit down;

offer something to drink;

make other appropriate offers according to Mr/s de Miguel's needs.

UNIT 9 **Dealing with salesmen/representatives**

1. Listening

Tapescript

SALESMAN A: Good morning. I'm Paul Richards from Isis Office Equipment. I'll only take a few minutes of your time.

CA: I'm Christine Adams. I'm afraid you've come at rather a bad moment: I'm expecting a visitor in about five minutes.

SALESMAN A: Five minutes will be fine. May I ask you who your main office supplier is?

CA: Well, we buy from various sources, but Arco supplies most of our equipment.

SALESMAN A: A very fine company. Well, at least now I know who our main competitor is here. Anyway, I'd like to tell you about some special deals. First of all, do you use ring binders?

CA: We do, yes.

SALESMAN A: Well, we have a good range of ring binders. These here are particularly popular. They're strong, and we have a good range of colours, as you can see from the catalogue. We have a special offer on at the moment which makes them very attractive at only 93p each.

CA: I'm afraid we don't need any at the moment, but I'll bear them in mind. But that reminds me of something we do need. How about desks? Do you stock any desks?

SALESMAN A: Yes, we certainly do. They're on page ... 35 of the catalogue. This one here is the most popular. We have a choice of three colours and the desk is larger than average.

CA: And what's the price?

SALESMAN A: OK, the normal price is £220, but as an introductory offer I can give you a 10 per cent discount ... making it £198. That's a very reasonable price.

CA: Well, I'll have to check with my boss before I place an order, but I'll bear it in mind.

SALESMAN A: We are selling photocopying paper at 60p per hundred sheets at the moment. That's cheap compared to normal prices, and it gives good reproduction.

CA: (*to phone*) Yes. OK, I'll be right over.

(*to SALESMAN A*) I'm afraid I'll have to leave you now. One of the secretaries will see you out. Thanks for calling.

CA: Hello, Christine Adams.

SALESMAN B: Hello, Mrs Adams. James Philby from Arco Office Supplies here.

CA: Hello, Mr Philby.

SALESMAN B: Mrs Adams, I just wanted to check that the last order arrived on time.

CA: Yes, it did. We are using the typewriters at the moment.

SALESMAN B: Good, I'm glad to hear that everything's OK. Last time we met, you said that you might need some more office supplies, so I thought I'd just check if there is anything else you need.

CA: One moment. I'll just get my notes ... Do you stock size B196 printer ribbons?

SALESMAN B: No, but we have a new ribbon in stock that will fit. They're only £2.65 each, which is a very attractive price; and they don't smudge.

CA: Fine. Can I order six?

SALESMAN B: Anything else?

CA: I am running out of filing space, so we may need to order another filing cabinet.

SALESMAN B: We are selling off some filing cabinets at £115 each. They're better than average quality too.

CA: And colour?

SALESMAN B: We have a choice of four colours. Oh yes! Last time you ordered some computer disks. Do you need any more?

CA: I'll have to check to see how many we are using.

SALESMAN B: At the moment we are stocking disks with more storage capacity and they don't corrupt.

CA: How much are they?

SALESMAN B: £12 for ten.

CA: Fine. I'll be in touch if we need anything.

SALESMAN B: Good. I look forward to hearing from you.

CA: Goodbye.

SALESMAN B: 'Bye.

Answers to the listening task

Company name: Isis Office Equipment		
Product	Offer price	Features
1. Ring binders	£2.93 each	(i) strong (ii) good range of colours
2. Desks	£198 each	(i) choice of three colours (ii) larger than average
3. Photocopying paper	60p per hundred sheets	(i) cheap (ii) good reproduction

Company name: Arco Office Supplies		
Product	Offer price	Features
1. Printer ribbons	£2.65 each	(i) very attractive price (ii) don't smudge
2. Filing cabinets	£115 each	(i) better than average quality (ii) choice of four colours
3. Computer disks	£12 for 10	(i) more storage capacity (ii) don't corrupt

3. Controlled practice

1. is causing
2. employ
3. are planning/plan
4. is asking
5. complain/are complaining
6. are trying
7. think
8. am trying
9. need

4. Transfer

(a) **Student B:** your partner is now going to tell you his/her normal duties in the company, and the present situation. Write notes in the table below.

Regular	Now

(b) Now tell your partner about your normal duties in the company (i.e. what you regularly do in your job). Then tell your partner about the present situation,

e.g. My boss normally gives me a lot of letters to type, but he is visiting a client abroad at the moment.

UNIT 10 Future engagements

1. Listening 🔘

Tapescript

KW: Hello, Karen Williams speaking.
 S: Got a call for you from abroad. It's a bad line, but I'm pretty sure it's Mrs Everett.
KW: OK, thanks. Hello, Karen Williams speaking.

AE: Hello, Karen. This is Alice Everett here.

KW: Oh, hello, Mrs Everett. How are you?

AE: I'm fine thanks. And you?

KW: Yes. I'm fine too.

AE: And how are things in the office? Any problems?

KW: No, everything is fine.

AE: Good, I'm glad to hear that. Actually, Karen, the reason I'm ringing is to sort out the arrangements for my visit to Manchester next week.

KW: Yes, Mrs Everett. I'll just go and get the file. Won't be a moment. . . . OK, I've got it in front of me now.

AE: Good. I'd like to go over the whole itinerary, so that I know what I'm doing, and can make a few notes.

KW: Right. I think I've got all the details now. And I've also made the travel arrangements.

AE: OK, let's start with the 19th. What time does my flight arrive at Manchester airport?

KW: It arrives at 9.30.

AE: OK, yes, that's early enough. And when am I meeting Mr Collins?

KW: You're due to meet him at 11.00 a.m.

AE: At 11.00, fine. And where is that?

KW: At your hotel, the International.

AE: Good. By the way, did you make sure that the International has a telex machine?

KW: I did, yes, and it has got one.

AE: Good. What time are we having lunch on the 19th?

KW: 12.30, and at Le Manoir restaurant.

AE: Fine, I've made a note of that. So that just leaves the afternoon. There's only one appointment, isn't there?

KW: Yes, you're going to visit the accountancy company . . . Brown & Partners. That's at 2.45.

AE: Oh, yes. I'm going to present our new accountancy package, and meet the senior partner. Is that all for the 19th?

KW: That's all. Shall we go over the 20th now?

AE: Yes, please.

KW: Well, your day starts at 10.00 a.m.

AE: Fine. And where?

KW: Back at Brown & Partners.

AE: Ah yes. I'm meeting the senior partners to discuss software development.

KW: That's right. And that meeting finishes at 12.00.

AE: Good.

KW: At 12.30 you are due back at the International hotel.

AE: I'm having lunch with Mr Collins? Is that right?

KW: Yes, that's right, and that's all.

AE: What about my return flight?

KW: Your flight leaves at 4.25. Flight BA 619 from Manchester airport.

AE: At 4.25. Fine. Now, I'd like you to send a letter and a telex to Mr Collins giving him all that information. As he is responsible for my visit he should have all the details in black and white. Please make sure that goes off today or tomorrow please.

KW: Right. Is that all?

AE: Yes, I think so. Thanks, Karen. So I'll be back in the office on Wednesday. If there are any problems, you can always contact me in Manchester.

KW: OK, Mrs Everett. 'Bye.

AE: 'Bye.

Answers to the listening task

19th October

Time	Place	Event
9.30 a.m.	Manchester airport	Arrival
11.00 a.m.	International hotel	Meet Mr Collins
12.30 p.m.	Le Manoir restaurant	Lunch
2.45 p.m.	Brown & Partners	Present new accountancy package

20th October

Time	Place	Event
10.00−12.00 a.m.	Brown & Partners	Meet senior partners/discuss software development
12.30 p.m.	International hotel	Lunch with Mr Collins
4.25 p.m.	Manchester airport	Departure

3. Controlled practice

2. I am starting my/the training course on 14th May in the morning.
3. The training course ends at 17.00 on 14th May.
4. I am going to the theatre with PD at 19.30 on 14th May.
5. I collect my new dress at 17.30 on 14th May.
6. I am going to discuss the training course with VE and ask for a rise on 15th May.
7. VE is going to say that she is going to ask MD.
8. On 16th May I am having an interview at PS.
9. On 17th May MD is going to chat with me about the future.
10. At 12 o'clock on 17th May I hand in my notice.

4. Transfer

Model letter

COMPACT SYSTEMS
96 Rosewall Drive, Southtown, SO3 4BT

Mr K Collins
Regional Co-ordinator
Impact Systems
43 Wythenshawe Road
Manchester M21 4QD

———— 19——

Dear Mr Collins

I have now finalised the details of my visit to Manchester next week. I am arriving at Manchester airport at 9.30 on 19th October. At 11.00 I am meeting you at the International hotel. We are going to have lunch together at Le Manoir restaurant. Then in the afternoon at 2.45 I am going to present our new accountancy package to Brown & Partners.

On 20th October between 10.00 and 12.00 I am meeting the senior partners at Brown & Partners, and we are going to discuss software development. We are having lunch together again — this time at the International hotel. Then I am leaving from Manchester airport at 4.25.

I look forward to seeing you on Monday.

Yours sincerely

Alice Everett
Marketing Manager

Model telex

```
ATTN: KEN COLLINS
FROM: ALICE EVERETT

RE: VISIT TO MANCHESTER 19 & 20 OCT.
CONF ARRIVAL M/C AIRPORT 9.30 ON 19 OCT.   MEET U INTERNATIONAL
HOTEL 11.00.   THEN LUNCH LE MANOIR 12.30.   VISIT BROWN & PARTNERS
14.45.
ON 20 OCT VISIT BROWN & PARTNERS 10.00 - 12.00.   MEET U FOR LUNCH
AT INTERNATIONAL HOTEL 12.30.   DEPART M/C AIRPORT 16.25.

RGDS
ALICE EVERETT
```

UNIT 11 Conference facilities

1. Listening 📼

Tapescript

  S: Bath Conference Information Centre.
HB: Good morning. I'd like to speak to someone in connection with conference facilities.
  S: Certainly. I'll connect you to our Information Officer, Mike Davies.
IO: Mike Davies speaking.
HB: Yes, good morning. My name is Hilary Beacham from Compact Systems. I'm calling to get some information about conference facilities.
IO: Well, first of all, can you tell me a little bit about what you're looking for?
HB: Yes. Well, I realise it's quite short notice, but we'd like to arrange a conference in Bath in November. It's our annual sales conference and there will be about 30 people involved. We will need two conference rooms and accommodation. Last year we arranged the meetings and the accommodation in different places. Apparently that wasn't very successful. So this year we'd like to find a hotel with meeting rooms where we can hold our conference.
IO: So you don't really need large conference rooms then, if you are only around 30.
HB: Yes, that's right. One more thing. Our Managing Director has already given me the names of four hotels and has asked me to check the details of those. So perhaps we could start with them.
IO: OK. Which ones have you got?
HB: Well, first there's the Hotel International.
IO: The Hotel International? I think you mean the International.
HB: Yes, I presume that's the one. Then there's the Regency.
IO: In fact it's called the Regent.
HB: OK. Thirdly, I've got the Bath Concord.
IO: Yes.
HB: And finally the Imperial.
IO: Yes, that's right.

HB: And do they all have conference facilities?
IO: Yes, they do, though some only have extremely large rooms — for more than 200 participants.
HB: I see.
IO: Well, apart from size, what exactly are you looking for in terms of facilities?
HB: Well, firstly the hotel must be fairly close to the airport.
IO: Well, the Regent and the Bath Concord are quite near the airport, but the Imperial is probably rather closer than the first two.
HB: And what about the International? Is that near the airport too?
IO: No, not really. However, it does provide easy access by road.
HB: Well, that's my second point — access by road.
IO: Well, I've already mentioned the International.
HB: So what about the other hotels in terms of road access?
IO: The Bath Concord is pretty easy to reach, but it isn't near the city centre. On the other hand, it does have a variety of large and small conference rooms. And the International is somewhat further out of town.
HB: What about the others?
IO: Well, the Imperial has only large meeting rooms, but it is very near the city centre.
HB: And the Regent? Is that near the city centre?
IO: No, not really. The Imperial is considerably closer to the city centre than the Regent. However, I should add that the Regent is very easy to get to by road — much easier than the Imperial. And the Regent offers both large and small conference rooms. In fact they have a slightly wider choice than the Bath Concord.
HB: And do any of them offer special rates in November? It's off-season, isn't it?
IO: Yes, it's off-season for tourists, but not for conferences. The Bath Concord and the Imperial don't offer any discounts. The International offers about 50 per cent off accommodation if you use the hotel's conference facilities.
HB: And the Regent?
IO: Yes, they offer a little more off accommodation, but their conference rooms are somewhat more expensive. . . . Anyway, to be honest I think it would be simpler if I sent you our booklet on conference hotels. Then you can see for yourself.
HB: Fine.
IO: And your address is?
HB: Compact Systems . . .

Answers to the listening task

	Hotels			
	1. The International	2. The Regent	3. The Bath Concord	4. The Imperial
large and small conference rooms	X	✔	✔	X
special rates in November	✔	✔	X	X
near the city centre	X	X	X	✔
close to the airport	X	✔	✔	✔
easy access by road	✔	✔	✔	X

3. Controlled practice

> Dear Guest,
> We are not only more exclusive than our competitors, we are simply much better. As we are very sure that you have already noticed, the Imperial is located in an extremely good position and is easier to reach than other large hotels. Of course we are quite big. Yet we feel that we still offer a very personal service to all our guests. And if we were smaller, your choice of facilities would be more limited. And so our motto is 'Slightly more expensive but considerably better'.

4. Transfer

■ PAIR WORK

Student B: you are arranging a conference in Bath for your company.
(a) Ring the Information Officer in the Bath Tourist Office and complete the table below with the information that the Officer will give you.

	1.	2.	3.	4.
Rooms				
Restaurants				
Distance to airport				
Meeting rooms				

(b) After you have completed your table, compare the hotels. In each case you feel that there is a big difference, e.g. 'So the Concord is much bigger than the Regent'. The Information Officer will disagree in his/her reply by saying that there is a moderate or small difference, e.g. 'Well, in fact the Concord is somewhat/slightly bigger than the Regent, rather than much bigger.'
Now you start as follows:
'So the Concord is much bigger than the Regent.'

(c) Finally, you must choose a hotel with the following facilities:
   (i) At least three meeting rooms
  (ii) At least 150 bedrooms
 (iii) At least three restaurants
 (iv) Not more than six miles from the airport
Discuss your requirements with the Information Officer, and choose one of the hotels.

UNIT 12 **Office talk**

1. Listening 🔘

Tapescript

KW: I've just run into that office designer chap . . .
HB: Mr Harris?

KW: That's right. Anyway, he had a pile of papers and a tape measure in his hands. What's going on? Do you know, Hilary?

HB: Well, I'm not supposed to tell you, but ...

KW: This sounds interesting! Go on.

HB: We're going open plan.

KW: Does that mean we're going to be sharing a room with the bosses?

HB: No, not exactly, but we're going to share the office with some of the other secretaries. It's all part of the new development, but the bosses haven't agreed on the details yet. Talking of secretaries, there's a new girl in Finance. I've just met her. Have you seen her yet?

KW: No, I haven't. What's she like?

HB: She seems nice, but very quiet. Probably just settling in. We're going out for lunch together.

KW: That's good. Make her feel more at home. What's her name?

HB: Shirley Lewis.

KW: Shirley Lewis! Well, if it's the same one, we're old friends. I've known her for years. Anyway, I suppose that with the new extension going up, there will be some more jobs going here at Compact.

HB: Yes. I mean have you seen the plans?

KW: Yes, it's going to be huge.

HB: Well, I haven't seem them, but I've heard they want to move all the departments around ... By the way, Karen, I need to check when you are taking your holidays. It's soon, isn't it?

KW: Yes, in two weeks, actually.

HB: I must arrange to get a temp in. Are you going on your own?

KW: No, with my sister. We're going to Paris. We haven't had a holiday together since we were kids. I've never been to Paris before, so I'm trying to find out where the nicest places are. Have you been?

HB: Yes, but ... let me think ... In fact, I haven't been since 1983 ... but Paris is wonderful.

KW: I've been to Brittany before, but never to Paris. Brittany's very nice.

HB: You do lead a busy life − what with holidays and then moving. That's going to be soon, too, isn't it?

KW: Well, we've already packed everything up, but the actual move will be just after we come back from Paris. But I've heard that you're moving too, Hilary.

HB: Well, actually we've decided to wait for a while before we sell our house. We probably won't be moving until September. (*pause*)

KW: Well, I suppose it's about time I got back to work.

HB: Good idea. Now, what did I come in for? Oh yes, have you found that file on Bovis yet?

Answers to the listening task

	Hilary	Karen
Met the new secretary in Finance	✔	X
Seen the plans for the new extension	X	✔
Been to France	✔	✔
Moved house	X	X

3. Controlled practice

(a)
2. I've already sent off the new report.
3. I haven't typed up the minutes of the last meeting yet.
4. Karen has already circulated the agenda for the next meeting.
5. Karen hasn't sent the timesheets to Personnel yet.
(b)
2. Have you checked today's correspondence yet?
3. Has Karen brought the new catalogue yet?
4. Has the Managing Director decided when the office staff will move yet?
(c)
2. Has Compact sold products to the US for three years?
3. Has Compact been in these premises since August 1985?
4. Has Michael Stott worked as Production Manager for two years?
5. Has the company grown by 15% p.a. since it was set up?

4. Transfer

■ PAIR WORK

Student B: you are a new secretary who has recently joined student A's company. Below are the things that you should do in the first month. It's now the end of the first month. Your partner is going to check how you have got on. Use the information given below to answer the questions.

Actions	*Present situation*
Met the managers	Met Production and Marketing Managers
Read the office rules and regulations	Read about half: 10 pages
Studied the word-processing manual	Nearly finished
Seen all the departments	Production/Marketing
Bought meal tickets for next month	Only for two weeks
Received details of the company sports facilities	Swimming/aerobics
Joined any of the company clubs	No

Your partner will start like this:

Student A:
Have you met all the managers yet?
Student B:
Well, I've only met the Production and Marketing Managers.
Student A:
So you haven't met the Finance and Personnel Managers yet?
Student B:
No, I haven't.

Now your partner will continue.

UNIT 13 Communications

1a. Reading

Answers to the reading task

1. c
2. e
3. a
4. b
5. d

1b. Listening

Tapescript

HB: Helen, can you find me the file on Impex, please?
HW: Certainly, I'll do it right away.
HB: And Helen, would you mind bringing me a cup of coffee? All this paperwork is making me very thirsty!
HW: No, of course not. It's milk and one sugar, isn't it?
HB: That's right. I'm very grateful. By the way, how was your weekend? You went away, didn't you?
HW: That's right. I went to York with friends. It was very nice.
HB: Oh, I'm glad to hear you had a good time. Oh, by the way, before I forget, would you ask Alan Ford to pop in for a moment, please?
HW: Can't, I'm afraid. He's off sick today.
HB: Oh dear. That leaves me with a problem.
HW: Anything I can do?
HB: I don't know. I've got a pile of papers that need to be looked over before Monday. Could you work late tonight?
HW: I'm sorry, I can't. I've got friends coming round tonight.
HB: Oh dear!
HW: I'm terribly sorry.
HB: Never mind. What about tomorrow night?
HW: I'm busy tomorrow night as well. I'm so sorry.
HB: It's quite all right. Can you ask Karen to come in, please?
HW: Yes, of course.
HB: Oh, and would you tell her to bring that Impex file with her?
HW: Yes, of course.
HB: Thank you very much.
KW: Yes, Hilary. Here you are.
HB: Is that the Impex file?
KW: Yes.
HB: Thank you. And would you mind doing a quick letter for me?
KW: No, not at all.
HB: And make sure it goes first class.
KW: Certainly.

HB: Now, the letter is to Peter Reinhard, that is R−E−I−N−H−A−R−D, and the address is ...

Answers to the listening task

Request	Reply
1. Find the file on Impex	✔
2. Make a cup of coffee	✔
3. Ask Alan Ford to pop in	X
4. Work late tonight	X
5. Work late tomorrow night	X
6. Ask Karen to come in	✔
7. Tell Karen to bring the Impex file	✔
8. Write a quick letter	✔

3. Controlled practice

(a)
1. We would be grateful if you could send payment as soon as possible.
2. I would be obliged if you could phone on Monday morning.
3. We would appreciate if your Sales Department could return the samples.
4. I am writing to request a copy of this year's price list.

(b)
1. Could you send our current price list to Brown & Partners? (c)
2. Could you give the report on the Manchester visit to the Managing Director? (d)
3. Would you mind asking Karen Williams to show me copies of the correspondence? (e)
4. Would you ask Helen Wright to file away the notes on the meeting with Collins? (b)
5. Would you mind asking Helen Wright to check the arrangements for my visit to Switzerland? (a)

4. Transfer

Tapescript

AE: ... the letter is to Peter Reinhard, that's R−E−I−N−H−A−R−D, and the address is: 116 Grosvenor Road, Manchester. Now, start with 'Dear Peter'. No, change that to 'Dear Mr Reinhard'. Reference order number 9200CF3. Thank you for your letter of 23rd March, enquiring about receipt of the component parts for our TK100 computer, which were delivered on 3rd March. I apologise for the delay in replying, but before we can send payment we would be grateful if you could explain why at least 30 units out of a consignment of 120 were damaged on arrival. It seems that the damage was the result of faulty packing. I would therefore be much obliged if you could credit us for the faulty items. I look forward to hearing from you. Yours sincerely, A. Everett, Marketing Manager.

Letter

```
                        COMPACT SYSTEMS
                96 Rosewall Drive, Southtown, SO3 4BT

Mr P. Reinhard
116 Grosvenor Road
Manchester                              Your ref: order number 9200CF3
                                        Our ref:  9200CF3

                                        17 April 19——


Dear Mr Reinhard

Thank you for your letter of 23rd March, enquiring about receipt of the component parts for
our TK100 computer, which were delivered on 3rd March. I apologise for the delay in replying,
but before we can send payment I would be grateful if you could explain why at least 30 units
out of a consignment of 120 were damaged on arrival. It seems that the damage was the result
of faulty packing. I would therefore be much obliged if you could credit us for the faulty items.

I look forward to hearing from you.

Yours sincerely



A. Everett
Marketing Manager
```

Model letter

```
                        COMPACT SYSTEMS
                96 Rosewall Drive, Southtown, SO3 4BT

Mrs Mary White
Witney Stereo Centre
56 East Street
Witney
Oxon                                    Your ref: PCB023
                                        Our ref:  PCB023/AB

                                        17 April 19——


Dear Mrs White

Thank you for your recent letter enquiring about our range of Zanuchi stereo systems.
Unfortunately your letter does not specify the exact model. Therefore I enclose details of the
three models we supply – Z90, Z99, or Z200.

If you decide to place an order we would be happy to offer you a 10 per cent discount on
accounts settled within 30 days. However, we regret to inform you that we could not supply
before the end of the month, as our earliest delivery date is 30 days after receipt of order.

I would therefore be much obliged if you could let me know which model you are interested
in, if you decide to place an order.

Finally I would be grateful if you could quote the above reference in all correspondence. Please
do not hesitate to contact me if you require any further information.

Yours sincerely
```

UNIT 14 Around town

1. Listing 🔲

Tapescript

HB: Hello? Hello.
PF: Pierre Farabolini speaking.
HB: Mr Farabolini, this is Hilary Beacham from Compact.
PF: Oh, hello Hilary.
HB: I've got some bad news for you. I've just checked with the airport, and I've heard that your plane will be delayed by about two hours.
PF: I see. Well, what do you think?

HB: Well, first of all, your taxi is due to arrive in half an hour.
PF: Well, I really don't want to spend all that time waiting at the airport. Could you book it a bit later?
HB: Yes, certainly.
PF: So, I think I'll go into Southtown and do a bit of shopping ... buy a few presents for my family ... Where's the best place to go to look at the shops?
HB: It's quite difficult to explain. Let me think. It'd be much easier if you had a map.
PF: Just a moment, I've got one in my pocket. (*pause ... rustle of papers*) Right.
HB: OK. In that case, I'll explain how to get to the town centre from the Cromarty. It's about a 15 minute walk, or you could go by taxi.
PF: No, I'm quite happy to stretch my legs.
HB: So, can you see the Cromarty on your map?
PF: Yes, I've got it marked.
HB: Well, you turn right out of the hotel and carry straight on for about 150 metres. Then you come to a roundabout. Take the first exit ... I mean go left.
PF: So, right out of the hotel. Then I go straight on until I come to a roundabout, and then I take the first exit.
HB: Yes, that's right. Then you walk along there for about another 200 metres, and then you come to another roundabout. There you go right.
PF: So I go to the next roundabout, and turn right.
HB: Yes. And then you carry on for another 200 metres and then you come to a third roundabout. There you go straight over the roundabout, and then take the first left.
PF: Hang on a minute. Let me just check that I've got that. I go to the next roundabout, go straight over, and then take the first on my left?
HB: Yes. Then at the next junction, turn right and then immediately left. And that's the beginning of the main shopping area.
PF: OK. Just let me go over that last bit. I carry on to the next junction, and turn left and then right?
HB: No, the other way round. At the junction you turn right and then left.
PF: OK. I've got it. Thanks very much.
HB: Oh, don't mention it. I hope you find something for your family. Oh yes ... I nearly forgot. I'll ask the taxi to collect you from the hotel at 5 o'clock.
PF: At 5. That's fine.
HB: 'Bye.
PF: 'Bye.

Answers to the listening task

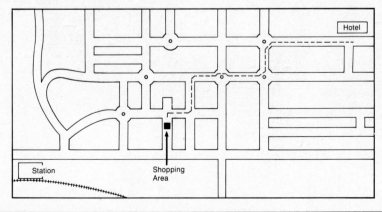

3. Controlled practice

1. Turn left out of the Cromarty Hotel and carry/go (straight) on. Take the third (on your) left. Then turn left and follow the road round to the right. The bank is in front of you.
2. Go out of the bank, and follow the road round to the left. Take the first (on your) right, and then turn right into Hamilton Street. Walk along there until you get to the roundabout and take the third exit. Bear left where the road divides and the sports centre is on your right.
3. Turn/go left out of the sports centre and take the first right. At the roundabout, take the first exit/go left. Natco is on your right opposite the garage.
4. Turn/go right out of Natco. At the roundabout take the third exit. The conference centre is on your left opposite Charlie's restaurant.
5. Turn/go right out of the conference centre and take the third exit at the roundabout. At the next roundabout go right/take the third exit. The Grosvenor Hotel is on your right opposite the railway station.
6. Turn left out of the hotel and take the third exit at the roundabout. Take the second (on your) left and then take the fourth exit at the roundabout. Take the first (on your) right, and then the first (on your) left. The post office is in front of you.

4. Transfer

■ PAIR WORK

(a) **Student B:** you are visiting a company in Southtown, and are staying at the Cromarty Hotel. You need to get to each of the following places tomorrow in the order given below.
    the post office
    Western Travel Bureau
    Maxi Supermarket
    Westco
Student A is a secretary in the company you are visiting. Ask for the directions for each of the above places in the order given above from the Cromarty Hotel. Draw your route and the position of each of the above places on the map below.

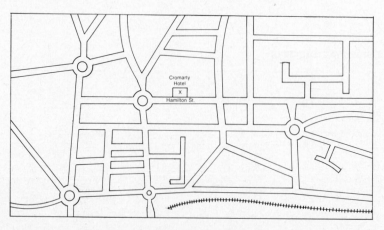

(b) **Student B:** first mark the following places on your map. You can put them in any position you choose.

National Bank
the railway station
Andy's restaurant
Northco

You work as a secretary in a company in Southtown. Student A is a visitor to your company. He/she is staying at the Cromarty Hotel. He/she needs to get to each of the above places tomorrow in the order given. Give him/her the necessary directions from the Cromarty Hotel.

UNIT 15 **Dissatisfied customers**

1a. Listening 🔲

Tapescript

HB: Hilary Beacham. Good morning.
PC: Could I speak to Alice Everett, please?
HB: Who's calling, please?
PC: My name is Paul Crown.
HB: And your company, Mr Crown?
PC: The company is Semantix.
HB: Sorry, could you spell that for me, please?
PC: Yes, that's S − E − M − A − N − T − I − X.
HB: Well, Mr Crown, I'm afraid Mrs Everett is away on business until next week. Perhaps I can help.
PC: Well, you can certainly make a note of my complaints.
HB: Could you explain the problem?
PC: Some time ago Mrs Everett suggested a link up between our two companies. At that stage I said I would like to see your product range.
HB: Yes.
PC: We arranged for one of your reps to visit me last week, but he did not turn up. I was naturally very annoyed.
HB: Yes, I understand. I'm very sorry to hear that. I'm sure there's a very simple reason for the misunderstanding.
PC: Unfortunately, Mrs ...?
HB: Beacham.
PC: There's more to come. When your rep had not shown up by 4.30, I telephoned your office to find out what had happened.
HB: Yes.
PC: And the secretary I spoke to was extremely rude to me. Again I was naturally very annoyed.
HB: I understand. Did you get her name?
PC: Unfortunately not.
HB: I do apologise, and I will try to find out who you spoke to and take appropriate action.
PC: Anyway, the reason I phoned her was to ask her to tell the rep to contact me and explain why he hadn't shown up. All I wanted was an explanation. Now that was over a week ago, and I've heard nothing.
HB: Well, Mr Crown, I'm extremely sorry to hear about your complaints. I can assure you that I will look into all of them immediately, and will get back to you as soon

as I have found out exactly what has happened. In the meantime, please accept my apologies.

PC: In that case, I will expect a call either from you or from the rep.

HB: Indeed.

PC: Goodbye.

HB: Goodbye.

Answers to the listening task

```
To: Alice Everett
From: Hilary Beacham

             While you were away
Name: Paul Crown    Company: Semantix
visited:            phoned: ✔
returned your call:   would like a call:

                  Message
Complaints:
1. Rep did not visit, as arranged.
2. Secretary was extremely rude.
3. Rep did not phone to explain why he did not visit.
```

1b. Reading

Answers to the reading task

```
Complaints:
1. no delivery of goods due two months ago
2. too late arrival of letter of explanation
3. two items missing from March order
```

3. Controlled practice

1. (c)
2. (e)
3. (g)
4. (h)
5. (a)
6. (d)
7. (f)
8. (b)

4. Transfer

(a) Speaking

Student B: you are Hilary Beacham. When Paul Crown's letter of complaint arrived on your desk, you decided to take immediate action in Alice Everett's absence. Below are your notes on Crown's complaints, your findings and your proposed action:

Complaint	Compact's finding	Agreed action
Late delivery of May order	Despatched last week	Offer discount (30%?)
Late arrival of letter of explanation	Postal strike	
Two missing items from March order	Warehouseman careless: sent 58 – not 60	Send two today

Now phone Paul Crown.
  Introduce yourself
  Explain the purpose of your call
  Present and apologise for each complaint
  Present your findings
  Present the action you will take in each case
  Make a final apology
  End the call

(b) Writing: model letter

COMPACT SYSTEMS
96 Rosewall Drive, Southtown, SO3 4BT

Mr P. Crown
Semantix
192 School Lane
Solihull
Birmingham

17th July, 19——

Dear Mr Crown

Further to my phone call earlier today, I should like to apologise again for the unfortunate events and to confirm the details of our conversation. As I explained, Mrs Everett is abroad; therefore I investigated your complaints.

Firstly, we are extremely sorry for the late delivery of your May order. I can assure you that it was despatched last week and will reach you very soon. Because of the inconvenience we are happy to offer you a 30% discount.

Secondly, I apologise that our letter explaining that the delivery would be delayed arrived late. This was unfortunately due to the postal strike.

Lastly, I regret that two of the items from your March order were missing. Unfortunately our warehouseman was careless and sent 58 instead of 60. The two remaining items will be sent today.

I should like to assure you that this will not happen again.

Yours sincerely

H. Beacham
Personal Assistant to Alice Everett

Work routines

---

1. Listening 🔘 ────────────────────────

Tapescript

HB: Karen, have you got a few minutes? I'd like to have a word with you.
KW: Yes, of course, Hilary.
HB: And is Helen around?
KW: Yes, she's just gone over to Finance. She'll be back in a minute ... oh, here she is now.
HB: Helen, could I have a word with you and Karen?
HW: Yes, of course.
HB: OK. Let's go into Alice's office. She's away today, and then we can talk a bit more privately.
HW: OK.
KW: OK.
HB: Right, now I've heard that the two of you have been complaining a bit ... about the extra work you are expected to do. So I thought we could perhaps discuss it and see if we can sort it out. Is that OK?
KW: Yes, it's a good idea.
HW: Yes, fine.
HB: OK, Karen, can you tell me what your problems are?
KW: Well, it's just that I can't manage to get through all my marketing work. I just seem to have too many other things to do.
HB: Go on.
KW: Well, first I often have to type letters for the departmental managers.
HB: You mean outside marketing?
KW: Yes, for Mr Ford, for example. When Cathy and Sally are too busy.
HB: I see.
KW: And then I sometimes have to type up minutes of meetings, which isn't really my job at all.
HB: No, that's right. That isn't your job. Anything else?
KW: Well, then there's the post. Occasionally I'm asked to sort through it.
HB: Do you ever have to distribute it?
KW: No, rarely. I mean Helen does that normally. I only do it when she's away or too busy.
HB: And how about dictation?
KW: Well, that's normally once a day, but that's not too bad because it's usually in marketing — so I don't mind. It's really all the other jobs that I get.
HB: I see, so the problems are mainly the letters — and typing the minutes.
KW: Yes, I suppose so.
HB: OK. Helen, what about you?
HW: Well, at the moment I always distribute the mail. But I thought it would be shared — not always me.
HB: I see. And what about sorting?
HW: Well, I do that twice a day, but it doesn't take very long. And anyway, that's part of my normal job.

HB: And what about meetings ... taking minutes or typing them?

HW: Well, I take minutes at the board meeting every month ... and again that's part of my job. But I'm also asked to type up minutes from other meetings.

HB: How often?

HW: I suppose I get some every week to type up ... and they're not from marketing.

HB: I see. And how about dictation and letters?

HW: Well, I suppose I do a dictation daily ... but it's often for other managers. I mean they just walk in and ...

HB: OK, Helen. I understand. And what about letters?

HW: I rarely type letters these days. I never have time.

HB: I see. So I suppose you just give them to Karen.

HW: Well, not exactly give them ...

Answers to the listening task

	Karen	Helen
sort through the post	occasionally	twice a day
take minutes at board meetings	———	every month
take dictation	once a day	daily
type up minutes	sometimes	every week
type letters	often	rarely
distribute mail	rarely	always

3. Controlled practice

(a) Definite frequency

2. The post is delivered twice a day.
3. The photocopier is serviced every three months.
4. Canteen tickets are sold once a week.
5. The telephones are checked annually.
6. The fire alarms are tested twice a year.
7. Training courses for new staff are held every month.

(b) Indefinite frequency

2. Compact employees rarely look at the notice boards.
3. Compact employees quite often eat in the company canteen.
   Compact employees eat in the company canteen quite often.
4. Compact employees sometimes work overtime.
5. Compact employees always take their full holiday entitlement.
6. Compact employees usually come to work by car.
7. Compact employees often retire at 65.
8. Compact employees are never made redundant.

UNIT 17 **The suggestions box**

1a. Reading

equipment	working procedures	general
2	1, 4	3, 5, 6

1b. Listening 🔘

Tapescript

HB: Alice, are you busy?
AE: As usual. But what can I do for you?
HB: I've just opened the suggestions box, and I wanted to have a word with you about some of the suggestions.
AE: OK.
HB: The first one is about the morning tea break. At present it's at 11.00, and the suggestion is to change it to 10.30.
AE: Well, and what do you think?
HB: I think we should have it a bit earlier, if that's OK.
AE: I have no objections at all.
HB: Good. The second one is about the printer.
AE: Another complaint about the noise?
HB: Afraid so.
AE: Well, we can't replace it. But it might be a good idea to fit a better cover so that it isn't as noisy.
HB: OK, I'll investigate. Right, the next one says 'What about having a non-smoking office?'
AE: A nice idea, but unfortunately unrealistic with so many people working in the same office. But why don't you talk informally to the office staff and see if the smokers can agree to smoke outside the office or something?
HB: OK, I'll do that. The next one is about flexitime. Don't you think we should consider it? Most of the other companies in Southtown have already introduced it.
AE: I'm afraid the Managing Director has already said no to that one, and I agree with him for the moment. I think we should look at it again next year.
HB: Fine. OK, just two more. How about a company Christmas party?
AE: Yes, I'm all in favour. We've got plenty of time if we start thinking about it now. Why don't you start planning after the summer?
HB: OK, I'll enjoy organising that. And finally, there's a suggestion about reorganising the furniture in the main office. The secretaries all say that they are very cramped. Don't you think we should do something about it?
AE: Yes, absolutely. It's been on my mind for quite a while now. I suggest that we have a word with Christine Adams, the Office Manager, and see what can be done.
HB: Good, that's all. Thanks very much.

144

Answers to the listening task

Suggestion	Agrees	Disagrees
1. tea break at 10.30	✔	
2. new printer		✔
3. non-smoking office		✔
4. flexitime		✔
5. company Christmas party	✔	
6. reorganising the furniture	✔	

3. Controlled practice

1. (b)
2. (a)
3. (c)
4. (a)
5. (b)
6. (c)
7. (b)
8. (b)

UNIT 18 The board meeting

1. Listening

Tapescript

DB: Good afternoon gentlemen, ladies. I do apologise for the slight delay — I will try to make up the time by carrying straight on to point 4 on your agendas — the annual marketing report. If we have time later we will return to the less important items on the agenda.
So, now for the marketing report. Alice Everett has just returned from Germany this morning, and has been working on a new set of up-to-date figures. So, Alice, over to you.

AE: Good afternoon. If I appear out of breath, it's because I've literally just arrived back, and the figures I am going to give you have just been presented to me and copied for this meeting. Perhaps you will allow me to go through the report first and then we can deal with any questions at the end.
The first thing to report is that Alan Ford, my Assistant Manager, has performed very well. As you know, he joined us exactly a year ago, and he's been a great asset to the department. He works very well with other members of the department and his enthusiasm in his work is commendable. I feel sure that our general increase in market share is partly due to his efforts.
Going on to specifics, as you know I spent two weeks in Germany in May this year, and in general we've made good progress there between 1985 and now.

145

In 1985 we had 26 per cent of the market. Not a bad proportion. We increased it by 3 per cent in 1986, reached 30 per cent in 1987 and in 1988 we managed to achieve 33 per cent. A significant increase, I'm sure you'll agree.

X: Very impressive figures.

AE: However, I'm afraid our performance in Spain isn't quite so good. We had 7 per cent of the market in '85, increased it by 2 per cent over the next year, and got to 12 per cent in 1987 ...

DB: That's still a very respectable performance.

AE: September, October and November of this year really saw the turning point.

Y: Can you give us some details?

AE: Certainly. Several important things have happened. Firstly, two other UK firms in our market have branched out into Spain and secondly, another Spanish firm has had a big marketing drive.

DB: What was the result?

AE: Well, we dropped by 2 per cent.

DB: Understandable under the circumstances. And what about France?

AE: Steady improvement: 13 per cent in 1985, an increase of 2 per cent in '86, a further 4 per cent the next year and finally we added another 2 per cent in 1988. I feel that we could do much better if our representatives are given the OK on the planned increase in expenditure.

DB: When do they need to know?

AE: They've been expecting a telex since yesterday.

DB: Let's discuss it later, shall we? And what about the domestic market?

AE: Steady progress again. The final figure is 22 per cent from a starting point of 15 per cent in '85.

Y: What about the intervening years?

AE: Well, we achieved 17 per cent in '86 and increased that by 2 per cent in 1987.

DB: Fine. If that's all, Mrs Everett, we can move on to the second item on the agenda: unit production costs. I would like to ask Michael Stott, our Production Manager, to give us his report. Michael ...?

Answers to the listening task

	UK	Spain	West Germany	France
1985	15%	7%	26%	13%
1986	17%	9%	29%	15%
1987	19%	12%	30%	19%
1988	22%	10%	33%	21%

3. Controlled practice

So, you have heard the highlights of our activities last year and the main details of our market plan for next year. In conclusion I would like to say that last year we made a good profit from our activities in South America. As a result we have consolidated our market position. In November I visited our subsidiary in Portugal, and I was very pleased with our staff out there. They have worked very hard to establish our products in the market. Mr Suares, the General Manager, showed me round the plant, and it was a very interesting experience. He has been in charge for nearly one year now and he has improved efficiency enormously. In fact I have just received a note from him, and it seems that last month's sales increased by another 12 per cent. So, things are looking good.

4. Transfer

Model letter

Mr R.V. White
103 Spalding Road
Chiswick
London

15 August 19——

Dr Mr White

I have been asked to write to you giving an account of last week's meeting.

The meeting began at 10.30 and the minutes were approved. After lunch at 1.00, there was a tour of the factory which started at 2.30 followed by a reception at a nearby hotel at 4.00. Dinner was at 6.00, and the members returned to their hotels at 9.00.

Now for some details about the South American market. The South American market has improved and South American profits have increased.

Finally, Mr Barry has asked about the report on the African market. Have you sent it yet?

I look forward to hearing from you.

Yours sincerely

UNIT 19 Considering job applicants

1a. Reading

Answers to the reading task

1. experience of working in a computer company
2. have good typing and shorthand
3. have a pleasant telephone manner

1b. Listening 🔘

Tapescript

S: Compact Systems. Good morning.
AW: Good morning. Could I speak to Hilary Beacham, please?
S: Who's calling, please?
AW: My name is Adel Wright.
S: Thank you. And what's it in connection with, please?
AW: The secretarial job advertised in last night's paper.
S: Thank you. One moment, please. I'm putting you through now.
AW: Thank you.
S: I'm afraid there's no answer. Would you like to leave a message?
AW: Uh, no, I'll ring back later. What time do you think she'll be in her office?
S: Well, if you give me your name, I'll tell her you're going to call.

AW: OK. It's Wright, spelt W − R − I − G − H − T. And the first name's Adel. That's A − D − E − L.
 S: OK, Miss Wright.
AW: It's Mrs Wright, actually.
 S: OK, Mrs Wright.
AW: So, what time should I call back?
 S: She'll definitely be in after lunch − at 2.
AW: OK. I'll call back after 2, then. Thank you.
 S: Bye.
AW: Bye.

 S: Compact Systems. Good afternoon.
AW: Good afternoon. Could I speak to Hilary Beacham, please.
 S: And your name is?
AW: Uh − Adel Wright.
 S: Thank you. And what's it about, please?
AW: The secretarial job advertised in last night's paper.
 S: Ah yes. You rang this morning, didn't you?
AW: Yes, that's right.
 S: Hold on a moment, please, Mrs Wright. I'll just connect you.
AW: Thank you.
HB: Hilary Beacham speaking.
AW: Good afternoon. My name's Adel Wright. I'm ringing in connection with the secretarial job advertised in last night's paper.
HB: Ah yes, Mrs Wright. You rang this morning, didn't you?
AW: Yes.
HB: Well, can I ask you a few questions?
AW: Of course.
HB: I presume you've worked in a computer company?
AW: Yes, I've had four years with DB Systems.
HB: Are you still there now?
AW: Yes, I am.
HB: I see. And what are your duties there?
AW: Well, I work in the sales department. I handle all the enquiries.
HB: I see. And are these written enquiries?
AW: Both written and phone calls.
HB: And do you have to do a lot of typing?
AW: No, in fact I use the phone for nearly all UK enquiries.
HB: And how about shorthand?
AW: Well, to be honest, it's a bit rusty.
HB: Good. So, perhaps you could tell me why you are interested in . . .

Answers to the listening task

Message
Date: 19 July 19——   Time: 11.30
For: Hilary Beacham
Mrs Adel Wright phoned. She'll call you after 14.00.

(3)

```
┌─────────────────────────────────────────────────────────────┐
│                    Notes on Applicants                        │
│                                                               │
│  Name: Mrs Adel Wright                                        │
│  Details: 4 years — DB Systems — sales department             │
│            Handles written and phone enquiries                │
│            Doesn't do a lot of typing                         │
│            Rusty shorthand                          (2)        │
│                                                               │
└─────────────────────────────────────────────────────────────┘
```

3. Controlled practice

1. (b)
2. (a)
3. (c)
4. (a)
5. (b)
6. (c)

4. Transfer

Student B: student A is trying to find his/her boss who is on a sales visit to the United States. In this activity you need to play a number of roles in a number of different American companies which student A is going to call in the search for his/her boss. You can be as helpful or unhelpful as you wish.

The order of companies is:

ABT (switchboard and PA/secretary to Joe Rondule);
Nova (switchboard and PA/secretary to Sales Manager — Paul Veritas);
Supra (switchboard and PA/secretary to Tony Armstrong);
City hotel in Detroit (receptionist).

Remember to:

identify your company and yourself;
ask for the caller's identification;
ask for further details;
connect the caller if possible;
provide any information you have;
suggest alternative action.

UNIT 20 **Organising the typing pool**

1a. Reading

Answers to the reading task

Causes	Effects
1. increase in business 2. backlog of work 3. we expect business to increase 4. the addition of a new secretary 5. this appointment	backlog of work in the production department problems in other departments we have appointed a new secretary improved efficiency in production backlogs in other departments

1b. Listening 🔲

Tapescript

CA: Good morning. I'd like to talk to you two so that we can discuss what will happen when Jo Cooper joins us next week. She is going to start on Monday, and because of this your responsibilities will be affected. Now, let's start with you, Jane. Because Jo is new to the company, I would like you to spend Monday and Tuesday showing her round. I'd like you to visit the personnel, marketing and finance departments on Monday, as I think it's important that she should get an idea of the company's activities. Is that OK?

JW: Yes, that's fine. Oh, just one thing. Taking newcomers around the departments can cause a bit of trouble.

CA: Yes, I know. I know what you mean. The best thing would be to warn the departmental heads. Then they can't complain.

JW: OK. I'll give them all a buzz, so that they know we're coming.

CA: Now on Tuesday I'd like you to show her the main purchasing procedures that you do here. Now I know that you've got a backlog of work and, as a result, things are a bit chaotic, but I don't want you to frighten her.

JW: Oh, don't worry, Christine.

CA: OK, now let's see about you, Samantha.

SW: Right.

CA: On Monday and Tuesday Jane will be busy with Jo. So, I'd like you to look after the phone. Therefore you probably won't have time to deal with all the correspondence. Don't worry about that. We will be able to catch up the following week when Jo has started to work. Now I've already talked to you about reorganising the work of the department, and you said that the backlog of work mainly results from the great number of phone calls, especially in the morning. Therefore, I've decided that as from next week Jo will start looking after the phone.

SW: But won't she find it a bit difficult by herself?

CA: Yes, but what I thought is that she could answer the phone. If there is a problem or a question she can't answer, then she'll ask you, Samantha. Jane can then concentrate on the correspondence and paperwork since she won't need to worry about the phone.

SW: But how will that solve the problem of the backlog?

CA: Well, I expect that in 2 to 3 weeks Jo will learn enough to handle most of the phone calls herself. And so in about 5 to 6 weeks I reckon we will manage to clear the backlog. Is that OK?

JW: OK.
SW: Fine.

Answers to the listening task

Jo Cooper is new (C)
Jo will visit the main departments (E)

Taking newcomers around the
  departments (C)
backlog of work (C)
Jane will be busy with Jo (C)
Samantha will look after the phone (C)

backlog of work (E)
great number of phone calls (C)
Jane can concentrate on the
  correspondence and paperwork (E)

Jane will show her round (E)
It's important that she gets an idea of
  the company's activities (C)
a bit of trouble (E)

things are a bit chaotic (E)
Samantha will look after the phone (E)
she won't have time to deal with all
  the correspondence (E)
the great number of phone calls (C)
Jo will start looking after the phone (E)
she won't have to worry about the
  phone (C)

[cassette tape icon]

3. Controlled practice

(a)
1. I forgot to set the alarm clock. (C)
   I didn't wake up in time. (E)
2. I missed the bus. (E)
   I didn't wake up in time. (C)
3. I missed the bus. (C)
   I arrived late at work. (E)
4. My boss was very angry. (E)
   I arrived late at work. (C)
5. My boss shouted at me. (E)
   My boss was very angry. (C)
6. I shouted at my boss. (C)
   My boss shouted at me. (E)
7. My boss sacked me. (E)
   I shouted at my boss. (C)
8. I am unemployed. (E)
   I forgot to set the alarm clock. (C)

> (b)
> Last Monday I forgot to set the alarm clock. So/Therefore I didn't wake up in time. Because/
> As/Since I didn't wake up in time, I missed the bus. Because of this, I arrived late at work.
> So/Therefore my boss was very angry. Because/As/Since he was very angry, he shouted at
> me. So/Therefore I shouted at him. Unfortunately this shouting led to the sack. So now I am
> unemployed because/as/since I forgot to set my alarm clock.

Preparing the agenda

1. Listening 🔲────────────────────────────

Tapescript

AE: So, to start with we need a date for the meeting. Initially I thought Tuesday 11th September, but the MD has said he won't be available at all that day. So, let's go for Wednesday 12th September.

HB: And the starting time?

AE: Let's start at 2.30.

HB: And who is going to attend?

AE: Well, it's a management meeting so the distribution list is all departmental managers and the managing director.

HB: How many items have we got for the agenda?

AE: Well, *I've* got four. And then I've received some suggestions from the other managers. Those are on that piece of paper there. We'll have to see how many of those can be included with the time we have available. So, firstly, I'll present the European marketing effort.

HB: So what should I put on the agenda?

AE: Call that one 'Marketing report: European market'.

HB: Right — 'Marketing report: European market'.

AE: Now I think that'll take about 45 minutes with questions. We mustn't let it go on too long. Once we've discussed that, we'll go on to consider the Far East market. So put that down as the second point on the agenda: 'Marketing report: Far East market'.

HB: OK — 'Marketing report: Far East market'. And thirdly?

AE: Next we'll get onto the forthcoming advertising campaign. Oh, and before I forget, will you remember to get those advertising proofs out of the file for me and leave them on my desk, please?

HB: Certainly. So, what's the last thing on the agenda? By the way, what about this suggestion for an item on 'Review of market research activities'?

AE: Oh thanks, Hilary. Yes, we should try and include that. Right — put 'Review of market research activities' third.

HB: OK. That means that we'll take the advertising campaign fourth?

AE: Yes. So fourthly we've got the advertising campaign.

HB: What should I call it on the agenda?

AE: Let's call it 'Advertising'. No, 'Advertising campaign'. Have you got that?

HB: Yes, 'Advertising campaign'.

AE: The last thing I've got for the agenda is the computerisation of the market-research programme. But perhaps we can take the item on 'Investment in new equipment' fifth. Yes, let's do that. So, fifthly we've got 'Investment in new equipment'. OK?

HB: So, point 5 is 'Investment in new equipment'.

AE: So that just leaves 'Computerisation of the market-research programme' as my final point for the agenda. In fact I doubt if we'll have time for anything else.

HB: So finally we've got 'Computerisation of the market-research programme'.

AE: Yes. And then don't forget to add AOB. Then we can mention the other points that we haven't had time to discuss and decide when we are going to go over them.

Answers to the listening task

3. Controlled practice

Before we start the meeting I'd like to go over the order of business, as there will be a small change. To start with we are going to hear the minutes of the last meeting. Once we have heard the minutes, we are going to move on to the second/next point. However, we are going to leave the third/next point on your agendas till later in the meeting. That means the third/next item will be the programme for next year. Fourthly/next we are going to consider the third point on your agendas — the Marketing reports for Spain and Italy. Finally/last(ly) we are going to set the date of the next meeting.

I have decided to change the order of the items on the agenda. Because I feel that pay increases are uppermost in your minds, we will take that first. Second(ly)/Next, because of the problems we have had with illness I'd like to take arrangements for sick leave next/second. Then I'd like to return to the beginning, to the first point — changes in work schedules. That leaves us with the second point — 'no smoking' arrangements. And finally/last(ly) we will have a general discussion.

UNIT 22 Arranging deliveries to/from the factory

1. Listening

Tapescript

Call 1
  S: Good morning. Expo Packaging.
HW: Can I speak to Mr Fellows, please?
  S: Hold the line, please. I'll connect you.
 PF: Peter Fellows.
HW: Good morning. Helen Wright here, from Compact Systems.
 PF: Good morning.
HW: I'm ringing to ask you when our order will be delivered.

PF: What's the order number, please?
HW: Just a minute — B153/2.
PF: I'll just find that file. Here we are. It's 50 packing boxes, isn't it?
HW: That's right.
PF: Yes. They will be delivered at the end of the month.
HW: But I was told they would be here around the middle of the month. You see, we have a delivery going out in two weeks and the boxes are needed before then.
PF: Well, the earliest they can be delivered is Thursday 16th January.
HW: That would be fine. At what time can we expect them?
PF: Our van has got three deliveries to make in Southtown in the morning, so your boxes can be dropped off some time after lunch — say after 2 o'clock.
HW: That's fine. Thank you very much for your help.
PF: That's OK. Goodbye.
HW: Goodbye.

Call 2
S: Zenith. Good morning.
HW: Hello. Can you put me through to your Purchasing Department?
S: Just a minute, I'll connect you.
Z: Purchasing.
HW: Hello. Helen Wright from Compact Systems. I'm phoning to let you know when your consignment of microchips will be delivered by our transport department.
Z: I'm afraid the purchasing officer has just been called to the factory. Can I take a message?
HW: Of course. The order number is RC19, for 600 microchips.
Z: Fine. I've got that.
HW: We will get them to you on 21st January in the morning.
Z: Is that everything?
HW: Yes, thank you.
Z: Thanks. Goodbye.

Call 3
S: IMF. Good afternoon.
HW: Good afternoon. This is Helen Wright from Compact. Can I speak to David Hall, please?
DH: Speaking.
HW: Mr Hall, I'm ringing about a delivery of printer ribbons to Compact. They were ordered about a week ago and were expected today. Your van has just been here, but there's no sign of the ribbons.
DH: I'm very sorry about that. Well, let's see what can be done. They could be dropped off this evening if you need them urgently. Otherwise they can be delivered tomorrow morning.
HW: Can you just hold on while I check? Order number PR13/A is needed in production tomorrow afternoon at the latest. And it's for 500 ribbons.
DH: Er ... yes. As I said, they can be delivered either this evening or tomorrow 7th January.
HW: Tomorrow morning will be fine. So what time can we expect your van?
DH: Shall we say between 10 and 11?
HW: Good.
DH: My apologies for the mistake. Goodbye.
HW: Goodbye.

Answers to the listening task

```
┌──────────────────────────────────────────────────────────┐
│                    Phone Message Slip                      │
│                                                            │
│  Company: Expo Packaging        Called:    Was called: ✔   │
│  Goods: Packing boxes                                      │
│  Order number: B153/2                                      │
│  Quantity: 50                                              │
│  Delivery date: 16th January                               │
│  Time: after 2 o'clock                                     │
│  Message taken by: Helen Wright                            │
│  Date: 6 January     Time: 9.45                            │
└──────────────────────────────────────────────────────────┘
```

```
┌──────────────────────────────────────────────────────────┐
│                    Phone Message Slip                      │
│                                                            │
│  Company: Zenith               Called:    Was called: ✔    │
│  Goods: Microchips                                         │
│  Order number: RC19                                        │
│  Quantity: 600                                             │
│  Delivery date: 21st January                               │
│  Time: Morning                                             │
│  Message taken by: Helen Wright                            │
│  Date: 6 January     Time: 10.30                           │
└──────────────────────────────────────────────────────────┘
```

```
┌──────────────────────────────────────────────────────────┐
│                    Phone Message Slip                      │
│                                                            │
│  Company: IMF                  Called:    Was called: ✔    │
│  Goods: Printer ribbons                                    │
│  Order number: PR13/A                                      │
│  Quantity: 500                                             │
│  Delivery date: 7th January                                │
│  Time: 10–12.00                                            │
│  Message taken by: Helen Wright                            │
│  Date: 6 January     Time: 15.20                           │
└──────────────────────────────────────────────────────────┘
```

3. Controlled practice

(b) The hot plate for the canteen, which was ordered from the manufacturer one week ago, may be delivered in two weeks.

(c) The filing cabinet was loaded on the van this morning and will be delivered this afternoon.

(d) Fifty printers were ordered last Tuesday. They are urgently needed and must be delivered on time next Thursday morning.

4. Transfer

(a) Speaking

Student B: you work as PA/Secretary to Barry Okunwe, Managing Director of Niger Sea Transport in Lagos, Nigeria.

Student A phones you and asks to speak to Mr Okunwe. He is not available so you take a message, which you write on the pad below. After you have completed the message, check the details with Student A.

```
┌─────────────────────────────────────┐
│              Message                │
│                                     │
│  From: _____                   │
│  To: _____                     │
│                                     │
│  Details:                           │
│     Order reference: _____     │
│     Goods: _____               │
│     Order placed: _____        │
│     Expected delivery: _____   │
│     Payment: _____             │
│     Action: _____              │
│     1. _____                   │
│     2. _____                   │
│                                     │
└─────────────────────────────────────┘
```

(b) Writing

Model letters for answer

(i)

Carnage Shipping Ltd
The Wharf
Southampton
England

Mr B. Okunwe
Managing Director
Niger Sea Department
Lagos
Nigeria

15 August 19——

Dear Mr Okunwe

re: Order B456/C

I should like to confirm the details of my phone call with your office today in connection with your order for three computers which was placed on 14 July. We expect that these will be delivered at the end of October. Our invoice is enclosed.

Your signature on the delivery conditions document is required. Therefore, I would be much obliged if this document could be signed by you and returned to us as soon as possible.

Yours sincerely

B. Wallis
Managing Director

(ii)

Niger Sea Transport
Lagos
Nigeria

Mr B. Wallis
Managing Director
Carnage Shipping Ltd
The Wharf
Southampton
England

25 August 19——

Dear Mr Wallis

re: Order B456/C

Thank you for your letter of 15 August 19——. Your delivery conditions are accepted and the document has been signed and is enclosed. Payment will be made as soon as the goods are/have been received.

In addition, two more computers will be needed early next year. These can be discussed on my next visit to the UK.

Yours sincerely

B. Okunwe
Managing Director

UNIT 23 **Office equipment selection**

1. Listening

Tapescript

CA: Helen, I've got the list here of the new equipment for the main office. Can we just go over the details together one more time before I place the order? I want to make sure that I haven't made any stupid mistakes with my calculations.

HW: Yes, of course, Christine.

CA: OK, let's start with these filing cabinets. I want to make sure we're going to get the right size.

HW: Well, if you read out the specifications from the catalogue, I'll measure the ones here to check that they will fit.

CA: Right. The new ones are 132 cm high.

HW: That's exactly the same as this one. What about the width?
CA: That's 45 cm.
HW: Yes, that's identical too. And the depth?
CA: Er, the depth is 60 cm.
HW: Well, that's slightly deeper than our other ones, but it'll still easily fit into the space.
CA: So no problem there. We're OK on the filing cabinets. Now then. We're also getting a new printer but it must fit exactly into that space over there.
HW: Now let me see. It can be up to 75 cm wide. What's the width?
CA: That's OK, it's only 66 cm wide.
HW: How deep is it?
CA: Er, it's 41 cm in depth. Will that be OK?
HW: Yes, that's fine. Oh, it's got to fit under this shelf too. How high is it?
CA: Er, 30 cm in height.
HW: No problem. That'll fit perfectly.
CA: Now, the keyboard for the new word processor has got to go next to it here, so that it also fits under the shelf. Now that's also 15 cm high. So that must be all right in height.
HW: How is it in terms of width?
CA: It's 51 cm wide. Will it fit?
HW: Yes, just.
CA: And it's got to sit on the desk without wobbling. So how much depth have we got?
HW: The desk is 70 cm deep.
CA: That's fine then. The keyboard is 60 cm in depth. So we've got a bit of space over. Now, we are also replacing this desk, and I've got a feeling that the one I've chosen from the catalogue is slightly bigger than this one here. But let's see.
HW: This one's 115 cm wide, but we've got a bit of space here.
CA: Well, the new one's 124 cm.
HW: That'll be OK. It'll still fit in here. How deep is it?
CA: 65 cm.
HW: That's the same as this one. I presume the height is standard?
CA: Yes, they're all around 73 cm in height. Good. Now, lastly, there are the new partitions.
HW: Oh yes. We'll have a bit more privacy then.
CA: They're going to go here and here.
HW: Yes. And how big are they?
CA: 152 cm high and 185 cm long.
HW: I'm looking forward to those. Then I can really hide away from all the visitors!

Answers to the listening task

	Height	Length	Width	Depth
Filing cabinet	132	—	45	60
Printer	30	—	66	41
Word processor	15	—	51	60
Desk	73	—	124	65
Partition	152	185	—	—

3. Controlled practice

(a)
2. What size is the office?
3. How high is the window?
4. What is the depth of the drawer?
5. How big is the desk?
6. How wide is the window?

(b)
A: And we also sell a bigger filing cabinet.
B: Yes, I see. And how many drawers does it have?
A: This model has three drawers.
B: How high is it?
A: Well, the height is 140 cm.
B: And what about the depth?
A: It's 80 cm deep.
B: And how wide is it?
A: Let me see. Yes, it's 60 cm in width.
B: 60 cm? Well, in that case it's too wide/big to fit in here.

4. Transfer

Student B: you are an office equipment supplier, visiting Student A's company. You have got the following details of equipment from your catalogue.
　　Listen to the reasons for Student A's interest in your products.
　　Answer Student A's questions about available models.
　　Answer Student A's questions about dimensions and size.
　　Ask questions about the boss's office.
　　Discuss which items of furniture are most suitable (try and persuade Student A to take the asterisked model below in each case, because that gives you the most commission).

Desks

	H	W	D
Type A	0.8 m	2.2 m	1.3 m
Type B*	0.8 m	2.6 m	1.2 m
Type C	0.8 m	2.2 m	0.9 m

Book cases (a width of 1 m holds 100 catalogues)

	H	W	D
Type A*	1 m	1.5 m	0.3 m
Type B	0.7 m	2.0 m	0.3 m

Filing cabinets

	H	W	D
Type A	1.4 m	0.4 m	0.7 m
Type B	1.4 m	0.5 m	0.7 m
Type C*	1.6 m	0.6 m	0.9 m

UNIT 24 **The International Trade Fair**

1. Listening 🔘 ────────────────────────

Tapescript

S: Interfair. Güten Tag.

HB: Good morning. My name is Hilary Beacham from Compact in the UK. Can I speak to Frau Müller, please?

S: If you want to speak to Frau Müller you must phone this number — Munich 587224. What is it in connection with?

HB: The trade fair in Munich between 15th and 19th September.

S: If you hold on a minute, I'll see if Herr Bernstein is available. He is dealing with enquiries about that fair. Yes, I'm connecting you to Herr Bernstein now.

B: Bernstein.

HB: Good morning. My name is Hilary Beacham from Compact. We received some information two months ago about the trade fair in Munich from 15th to 19th September.

B: Yes?

HB: I sent our registration form on 1st August, but we haven't heard anything yet.

B: If your registration is correct, I will have the details here. If you give me the name of your company, I will check for you.

HB: The company is called Compact Systems.

B: Just one moment, please ... Did you enclose payment with your registration? You see, if you filled in your registration form correctly and sent payment, I would have your name on my list here.

HB: No, we didn't send payment, because we expected an invoice from you.

B: Mrs Beacham, then you didn't fill your registration form in correctly. The form clearly stated the conditions for registration, namely if you wanted a confirmed stand, you should send the appropriate payment. If you look at the forms, you will see it in black and white.

HB: Well, I'm sorry about the misunderstanding. So what can we do if we want a stand?

B: To be honest with you, you're a bit late. The closing date was last Monday.

HB: I see. But if we really wanted a stand, could you help us?

B: If you made your decision now, I could check the availability situation. If I found a free stand, you would have to let me know today.

HB: Can you check if you have a free stand?

B: Yes, certainly. Just one moment, please ... I've looked at the booking sheet and we've got a number of free stands.

HB: Where exactly are they?

B: There's one in the entrance lobby.

HB: If there was one in the main concourse, we would prefer that.

B: The main concourse — let me see. Yes, we have one there. But it's right at the end.

HB: Nothing in the middle?

B: Well, there's one company with a stand in the middle of the main concourse who haven't paid yet. If they don't pay today, and your bank telexes a transfer, I can let you have that.

HB: OK. So, if this company doesn't contact you today, can you call me before 17.00 UK time? If you call me I'll give you a decision immediately.

B: OK, Mrs Beacham. And your phone number is?

HB: Our phone number is ...

Answers to the listening task

	True	False
1. Interfair rings Compact		✔
2. Hilary Beacham asks to speak to Frau Müller	✔	
3. The trade fair is in September	✔	
4. Herr Bernstein isn't available		✔
5. Hilary returned her registration form	✔	
6. Hilary sent payment for a stand		✔
7. Bookings for stands are closed	✔	
8. Herr Bernstein has one free stand		✔
9. Hilary wants a stand in the lobby		✔
10. Herr Bernstein asks Hilary to phone before 5 p.m.		✔

3. Controlled practice

1. If you hang on I'll check for you.
2. If he was available he would talk to you.
3. If you ring at 16.00 he will be in the office.
4. If you don't call us we will call you.
5. If he spoke to you he wouldn't want to repeat everything.
6. If he didn't check he couldn't give you an answer.
7. If we send it today it will arrive tomorrow.
8. If you didn't send it it couldn't arrive.
9. If we had it we would let you know.
10. If the answer is yes you can start tomorrow.

UNIT 25 Two important phone calls

1. Listening

Tapescript

AE: Hello, is that Hilary?

HB: Yes, Hello, Alice. How are things going?

AE: Oh, hectic as always. Hilary, the reason I'm calling is because I need to find out how far you've got with the arrangements for the trip to Glasgow.

HB: Fine so far. What exactly do you need to know?

AE: First, the Hotel Regent in Glasgow. Have you managed to get me the dates I wanted?

HB: Not absolutely sure yet, Alice. They said they can probably fit you in on the 18th, the 19th, the 20th and the 21st. But then they've got a big party of Japanese coming. So they think they may be packed out. That means that it's unlikely that they can fit you in on the 22nd. But they've promised to let me know for certain tomorrow.

AE: And the conference centre?

HB: We've certainly got that from 2.00 to 9.30 on the 18th, and the 22nd should be all right, too. Oh yes, I've made a note here that the 21st is bound to be OK, too.

AE: Now, have you managed to contact the managers of the shops in Glasgow?

HB: Yes, I spoke to them this morning.

AE: And?

HB: They may make the meeting on the 20th, but I'm afraid they're unlikely to manage the 21st as well.

AE: OK. That's not too bad, then. Did you manage to contact our representative in Edinburgh?

HB: Yes, but he definitely won't be able to meet you on the 19th.

AE: That's really a pity. Can't be helped though. Now what about the restaurant?

HB: The 19th is likely to be OK, and I've definitely booked for the 22nd.

AE: Good. And now, what about the flights?

HB: I'm just going to check with the travel agents now.

AE: OK, I'll be back in the office tomorrow morning, so you can let me know about the flights then.

HB: OK. Fine.

AE: 'Bye.

HB: 'Bye.

TA: First Class Travel.

HB: Morning. This is Hilary Beacham from Compact. I'd like to check availability on the flights to Glasgow.

TA: When would you like to travel?

HB: Out − either the evening of the 17th or the morning of the 18th − and back on the 22nd.

TA: And how many seats?

HB: Just one.

TA: One moment, please ... OK. There are two evening flights on the 17th. 17.00 arriving 18.00; and 19.00 arriving 20.00.

HB: Yes. I've got that.

TA: And on the morning of the 18th there is one flight at 7.00 arriving at 8.00; one at 8.00 arriving 9.00; and one at 9.30 arriving at 10.30.

HB: And how about availability?

TA: For which flight?

HB: Could you check all of them, please?

TA: OK. One moment, please. ... I'm afraid there's a fault on the computer link, and the information is not absolutely up-to-date; it's last night's information. But it'll give you an idea.

HB: OK.

TA: Right. On the 17th I'm afraid the 17.00 is definitely full, so there's certainly no seat available on that flight. And the 18.00 − there was one seat left last night so that's likely to be full now too.

HB: I see. And what about the 18th?

TA: One moment, please. ... You may get a seat on the 7 o'clock − there were about 10 left last night. The 8 o'clock − let me see. Oh yes, plenty of seats left. I'm sure you'll get a seat on that one. And the 9.30 ... well quite a few seats left − so it's likely you'll get a seat on that one.

HB: OK. Let me go over that. On the 17th you are sure that the 17.00 will be full, and it's likely that the 18.00 will be full too?

TA: Yes, that's right.

HB: And on the 18th I may get a seat on the 7 o'clock, I'm certain to get one of the 8 o'clock, and I'll probably get one on the 9.30.

TA: Yes, that's right.

HB: And what about the return ...

Answers to the listening tasks

	True	False
The Hotel Regent can definitely fit Alice in from the 18th to the 22nd.		✔
The conference centre will certainly be available from 2.00 to 9.30 on the 18th.	✔	
The Glasgow managers are likely to make the meeting on the 20th.		✔
The Edinburgh representatives certainly can't meet Alice on the 19th.	✔	
The restaurant is likely to be available on the 19th.	✔	

	Seat available?				
	Definitely	Probably	Possibly	Probably not	Definitely not
Flight times – 17th Dep. 17.00 Arr. 18.00 Dep. 19.00 Arr. 20.00				✔	✔
Flight times – 18th Dep. 07.00 Arr. 08.00 Dep. 08.00 Arr. 09.00 Dep. 09.30 Arr. 10.30	✔	✔	✔		

3. Controlled practice

2. Brian may/might be in the office on Monday afternoon.
3. Chris is unlikely to be in Glasgow on Monday morning.
4. Derek is bound/certain to be available on Tuesday afternoon.
5. It is likely that Eric will be in Glasgow on Monday morning.
6. Allan definitely/certainly won't be available on Monday.
7. Brian will certainly/definitely be in the office on Monday morning.
8. It is unlikely that Chris will be available on Tuesday morning.
9. Derek may/might be available on Monday afternoon.
10. Eric is bound/certain to be in Glasgow on Monday afternoon.

4. Transfer

■ PAIR WORK

Student B: you are Personal Assistant to Mr/s Bryce (Sales Manager of a company). You are going to receive a phone call to arrange a meeting between Mr/s Bryce and Alice Everett (the manager of another company) for the week beginning Monday 21st August. Find out the best possible time for the meeting. Here is the relevant page from Mr/s Bryce's diary:

	a.m.	p.m.
Monday 21st	Meeting with sales reps (+ +)	New products meeting (+ +)
Tuesday 22nd	Trade fair in London (+)	Trade fair (?)
Wednesday 23rd	Japanese visitors (?)	Japanese visitors (+ +)
Thursday 24th		Meeting with Financial Director (+)
Friday 25th		Department meeting (+ +)

UNIT 26 End-of-year report

1a. Reading

Answers to the reading task

	True	False
The main cause of personnel changes is low pay.		✔
Many secretaries have left for better-paid jobs.	✔	
Alice Everett does not want to hold a pay review.		✔
There have been several negative responses to the questionnaire.		✔
Much useful information was gained from the questionnaire.	✔	
None of the replies were interested in the product.		✔
The conference went very well.	✔	
Most of the discussion was about China.		✔
Some of the company's products have been unsuccessful.		✔

1b. Listening

Tapescript

AE: Hilary, have you got a moment?

HB: Yes, of course.

AE: I've got the draft end-of-year report for marketing here. Karen has just typed it up, but I'd like to make a few changes.

HB: OK.

AE: Can I tell you the changes, and then you can ask Karen to edit it on the word processor?

HB: Yes, of course.

AE: In this first sentence of the first section, I don't like 'many personnel changes'. It sounds as if people are leaving every day. Can you change it to 'some'?

HB: OK.

AE: In the second sentence of the second section — have you got it?

HB: Yes ... starting with 'In brief'?

AE: Yes, that's right. Well, the responses to the questionnaire were very positive. So can you change 'a lot of' to 'most of'?

HB: Yes, I've got that.

AE: OK. Now the third section. In the second sentence there about trade with Europe?

HB: Yes, I can see it.

AE: Well, it wasn't 'much of the discussion'; it was 'most of the discussion'.

HB: OK. I've changed that.

AE: Section 4 is fine. I think we've all had a most successful year, don't you?

Answers to the listening task

1. Personnel in the Marketing Department
We have seen some personnel changes in the Marketing Department ...
2. Market research
None of the responses were negative and most of them gave very useful information.
3. Annual conference
Most of the discussion focused on trade with European countries ...

> **COMPACT SYSTEMS**
> **96 Rosewall Drive, Southtown, SO3 4BT**
>
> Dear Investor,
>
> I am sure that most of you will already have read in the papers that this year has been another good year for Compact. Without exception, all (of) our products have performed well in Europe — some of them, of course, better than others. From modest beginnings with only a few salesmen, we now have an extensive sales force both in the UK and abroad. As a result we now cover most European countries, and hope to extend our activities to the Far East in the near future. In order to make our whole selling team more effective we intend to give all of them an opportunity to improve their sales techniques. Some will follow training courses in Southtown, and others will be sent to centres in London. So, as you can see, a lot of/much money will be invested in training in the future.
>
> We had a few small problems at our Southtown factory early in the year due to delayed deliveries from the Far East which none of us could have foreseen. However, I am glad to inform you that they have now been resolved.
>
> We look forward to another successful year.
>
> *David Burton.*
>
> David Burton
> Managing Director

Telephone language

The following sentences and expressions will help you when making and answering phone calls. This appendix is divided into two sections:

outgoing calls (when you make the call)

incoming calls (when you receive the call)

Outgoing calls

Identifying yourself
My name is _____ (first introduction).
This is _____ here.
This is _____.

Asking to speak to someone
Could I speak to _____, please?
Could you put me through to _____, please?
Could I have extension 4356, please?
I'd like to speak to _____, please.

Giving further information
It's in connection with _____.
It's about _____.

Explaining purpose of call
I'm calling to ask about _____.
I'm phoning to let you know the details of _____.
I'm ringing to tell you about _____.

Showing understanding
I see.
I understand.

Leaving a message
Could you give _____ a message?
Could you ask _____ to call me (when he gets back)?
(Could you tell _____) I'll call back later.

Thanking
Well, thank you very much for your help.
Well, thanks for the information.
I'm very grateful for your assistance.
I'm much obliged to you.

Ending the call
I look forward to seeing/hearing from/meeting you.
Goodbye.
'Bye.

Incoming calls

Identifying your company (from the switchboard)
Compact Systems. Good morning/afternoon.

Identifying yourself when you pick up the phone
Hilary Beacham.
Hilary Beacham speaking.

Helping the caller
Can I help you?
Who would you like to speak to?
Which department is he/she in?

Asking for the caller's identification
Who's speaking, please?
Who's calling, please?
Which company are you from?

Asking for further information
What's it in connection with, please?

Connecting the caller
Just a minute/moment/second, please.
Hold/hang on, please.
Hold the line, please. I'll put you through.
I'm putting you through now.
I'm connecting you now.
You're through now.

Explaining that someone is not available
I'm afraid _____ is not available this morning/afternoon.
I'm afraid _____ is out at the moment.
I'm sorry, but _____ is on holiday/in a meeting at the moment.
I'm sorry, but _____ is on the other line at present.
I'm afraid his/her line's engaged. Do you want to hold?

Alternative actions
Could you ring/phone/call back later?
Would you like to leave a message?
Can I take a message?

Responding to thanks
Not at all.
Don't mention it.
You're welcome.

Ending the call
I look forward to seeing/hearing from/meeting you.
Thanks for calling.
Goodbye.
'Bye.

Telex abbreviations

Today telexes look more and more like letters, and letters look more and more like telexes. As a result telex abbreviations are not as common or necessary.

The following list of telex abbreviations is divided into two sections:

Standard telex abbreviations that you can use or may receive in the text of telexes.

Standard telex abbreviations used internationally by switchboard operators that you may receive.

1.
ANS	answer
ARR	arrive/arrival
ASAP	as soon as possible
ATTN	for the attention of
CFM	confirm
DEP	depart/departure
ETA	estimated time of arrival
ETD	estimated time of departure
INFO	information
NO	number
PLS	please
RE	about/referring to
RETEL	about telex ...
RGDS	regards
RPT	repeat
TEL	telephone
TELCON	telephone conversation
TKS	thanks
TLX	telex
URTEL	your telex

2.
ABS	absent subscriber, office closed
BK	I cut off
CFM	I confirm
DER	out of order
DF	you are in communication with the called subscriber
EEE	error
INF	subscriber temporarily unobtainable; call the Information (Enquiry) Service
MOM	wait/waiting
NA	correspondence to this subscriber is not admitted
NCH	subscriber's number has been changed
NP	the called party is not, or is no longer, a subscriber
NR	indicate your call number/my call number is ...
OCC	subscriber is engaged
PPR	paper
R	received
RAP	I will call you back
RPT	repeat/I repeat
SVP	please

TEST/MSG	please send a test message
THRU	you are in communication with a Telex position
TPR	teleprinter
WRU	who is there?

APPENDIX 3 **Abbreviations**

The following general business abbreviations may be used or found in written communications including letters, telexes, memos, notes and reports.

approx.	approximate/about
asst	assistant
avg.	average
bkg	banking
bldg	building
ca. or c.	circa/about
c.c.	carbon copy
cf.	compare with, compare
cont.	continued
contd	continued
dbl.	double
e.g.	for example
encl.	enclosed
esp.	especially
est.	established
et al.	and others
etc.	etcetera/and so on
excl.	excluding
ext.	extension
G.M.	General Manager
H.Q.	Head Quarters
i.e.	in other words/that is to say
incl.	including
intl.	international
max.	maximum
mfg	manufacturing
mfr	manufacturer
mgr	manager
min.	minimum
misc.	miscellaneous
mtg	meeting
N.B.	take special note of
p.a.	per year
p.c.	per cent
pp.	pages
P.S.	postscript
recd	received
R.S.V.P.	please reply
sec.	secretary
sgl.	single
std	standard
viz.	namely/that is
yr	year
yrs	yours

APPENDIX 4 Letters

Business letters are an essential part of making and confirming transactions in the commercial world. They are important in creating a good impression, and therefore *what* is written is as vital as *how* it is presented. There are various styles appropriate to business letters. These must take into account:

the company's letter head;

the company's in-house writing style;.

In addition the style of letters is constantly changing in line with different international business practices and new language developments. However, a good business letter should aim to be:

precise;

concise;

accurate;

The following are examples of five types of business letters:

a letter of application;

a letter of request;

a letter of reply;

a letter of order;

a letter of complaint.

1. A letter of application

63 Wenwell Gardens
Southtown
SO9 7PX

The sender's address ——→

Inventor Plus —— *The addressee*
60 Chiswick Avenue
Southtown
SO3 6QZ

10 January 19—— ←———— *The date*

The greeting (where the addressee's name is not known)

Dear Sir/Madam ←

The first paragraph says why you are writing

I am writing in response to your advertisement for a Personal Assistant/Seretary to the Managing Director.

The second paragraph gives further details.

I am enclosing a copy of my curriculum vitae, which gives details of my qualifications and experience. As you will see I have had 7 years' experience of working in a business environment and have an RSA 2 in Typing and Shorthand. Although I did not have to travel in my previous job, I would be very willing to do so.

I will be available for interview at any time, and look forward to hearing from you.

The final paragraphs includes a polite ending

Yours faithfully

The farewell (after Dear Sir/Madam)

Hilary Beacham

The signature

Hilary Beacham ← *The person writing the letter.*

2. A letter of request

Softchain Ltd ← *The letterhead includes the name and address of the sender.*
(Head Office), Foss House, Brigham Street, Liverpool L13 4AT
Tel: 051-387 6397   Telex: 79284

Compact Systems ← *The addressee*
96 Rosewall Drive
Southtown
SO3 4BT

Your ref:
Our ref: Inq. B7693 ← *The sender's reference*

5 April 19—— ← *The date*

Dear Sirs ← *The greeting (where the addressee's name is not known)*

The first paragraph says why you are writing

We recently attended the Software Trade Exhibition in Bath, and were impressed by the range of software available through your company.

The second paragraph gives the real reason for writing

We are a large chain of business software retailers and are looking for a software house which could supply us with a range of business applications programs.

As we usually place large orders, we would expect a quantity discount in addition to a 20 p.c. trade discount off net list prices. Our terms of payment are normally 30 days after receipt of invoice.

If these conditions are of interest to you, we would be much obliged if you could send us your current catalogue and price-list.

The final paragraph is a polite ending

We look forward to hearing from you soon.

Yours faithfully ← *The farewell (after 'Dear Sirs')*

pp. *Pat Miles* ← *The signature*

The person writing the letter

P. Barker ←
Purchasing Manager ← *The writer's position in the company.*

pp means that Pat Miles signed the letter for P. Barker

172

3. A letter of reply

COMPACT SYSTEMS

96 Rosewall Drive, Southtown, SO3 4BT

Tel: 0927-423845   Telex: 69364

Mr P. Barker
Purchasing Manager
Softchain Ltd
Foss House
Brigham Street
Liverpool
L13 4AT

Your ref: Inq. B7693
Our ref: AE/677

The addressee's reference

Alternative position for the date

10 April 19——

Dear Mr Barker ◄——————— *The greeting (where the addressee's name is known)*

Thank you for your letter of 5 April 19—— in which you asked details of our range of business applications programs.

Because of the low price of our software we do not normally offer a quantity discount; however, if you can give me an indication of the quantity involved, I would be happy to discuss terms further with you. Normally, we would be happy to offer you a 20 p.c. trade discount off net list prices, as requested in your letter, and to accept your terms of payment.

I am enclosing a copy of out most recent catalogue which gives details of our product range, together with list prices. I hope that the information will be of interest to you, and look forward to discussing orders in the near future.

Yours sincerely ◄——————— *The farewell (after a named addressee)*

p.p. *Hilary Beaucham*

Alice Everett
Marketing Manager

The enclosed documents

Encl. Compact catalogue, trade price list

'Encl. means enclosure(s)

173

4. A letter of order

Softchain Ltd
(Head Office), Foss House, Brigham Street, Liverpool L13 4AT
Tel: 051-387 6397   Telex: 79284

Mrs A. Everett   Your ref: AE/677
Compact Systems   Our ref: Ord. B7693
96 Rosewall Drive
Southtown
SO3 4BT

15 July 19——

Dear Mrs Everett

Please find enclosed our order, Ord. B7693, for 100 IBM compatible Compact Accounts packages, as discussed in our phone conversation of 12 July.

We have decided to place an order for 100 packages and accept the 20 p.c. trade discount off net list prices as discussed. Payment will be made, as agreed, 30 days after receipt of your invoice.

We would be much obliged if you could despatch the goods so that they reach us no later than 30 July, and look forward to receiving your acknowledgement.

Yours sincerely

P. Barker

P. Barker
Purchasing Manager

Encl. Ord. B7693

---

5. A letter of complaint

Softchain Ltd
(Head Office), Foss House, Brigham Street, Liverpool L13 4AT
Tel: 051-387 6397   Telex: 79284

Mrs A. Everett   Your ref: AE/677
Compact Systems   Our ref: Ord. B7693
96 Rosewall Drive
Southtown
SO3 4BT

2 August 19———

Dear Mrs Everett

On 15 July we placed an order for 100 IBM compatible Compact Accounts packages. A consignment was delivered on 30 July, but upon inspection we found that the packages were not IBM compatible.

As this is our first transaction with your company we are naturally disappointed that we have got off to such a bad start. Therefore I would be much obliged if you could send us the correct goods as soon as possible, and arrange for the collection of the incorrect ones.

Yours sincerely

P. Barker

P. Barker
Purchasing Manager

Vocabulary index